This Book Belongs To

Color Test Page

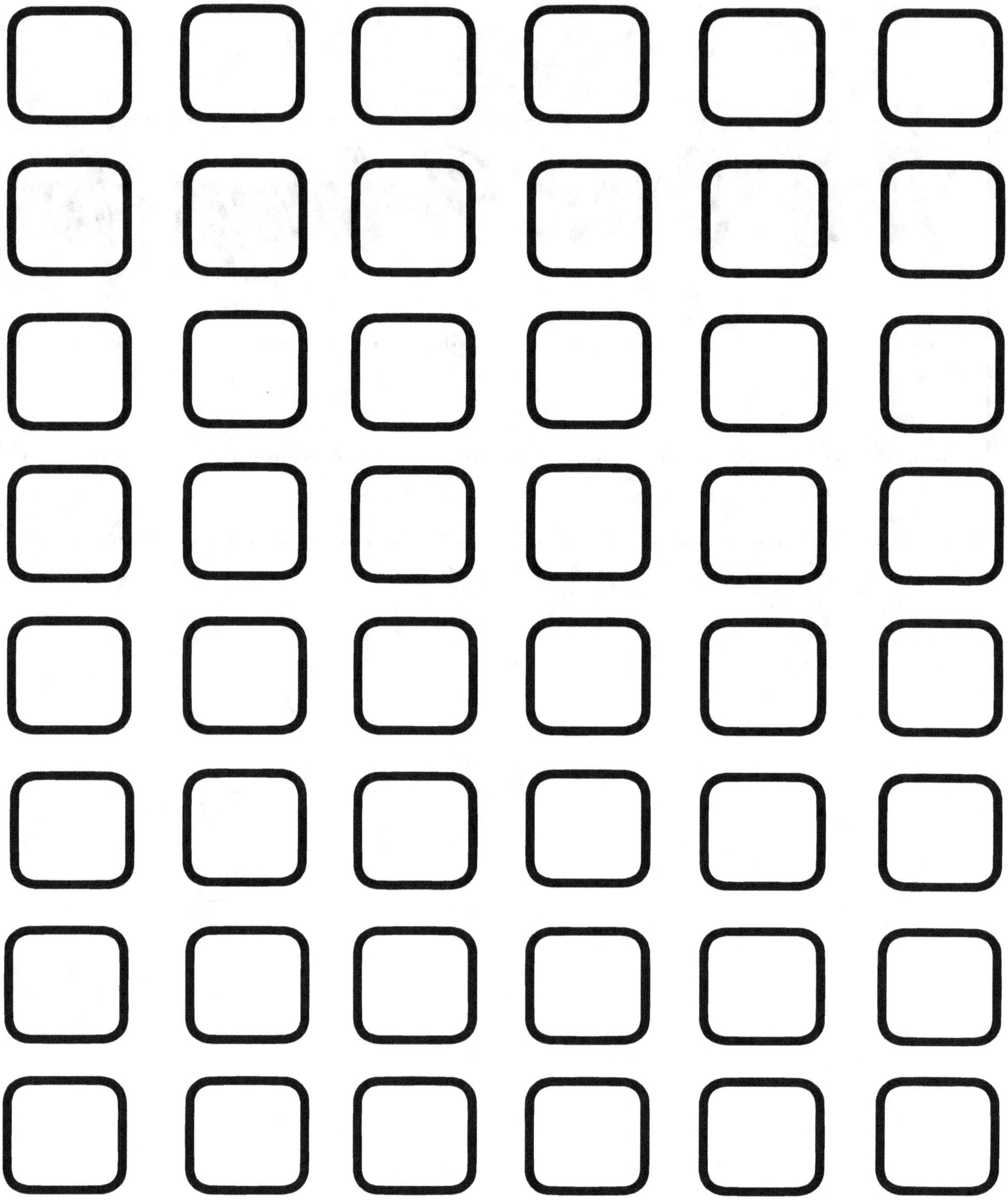

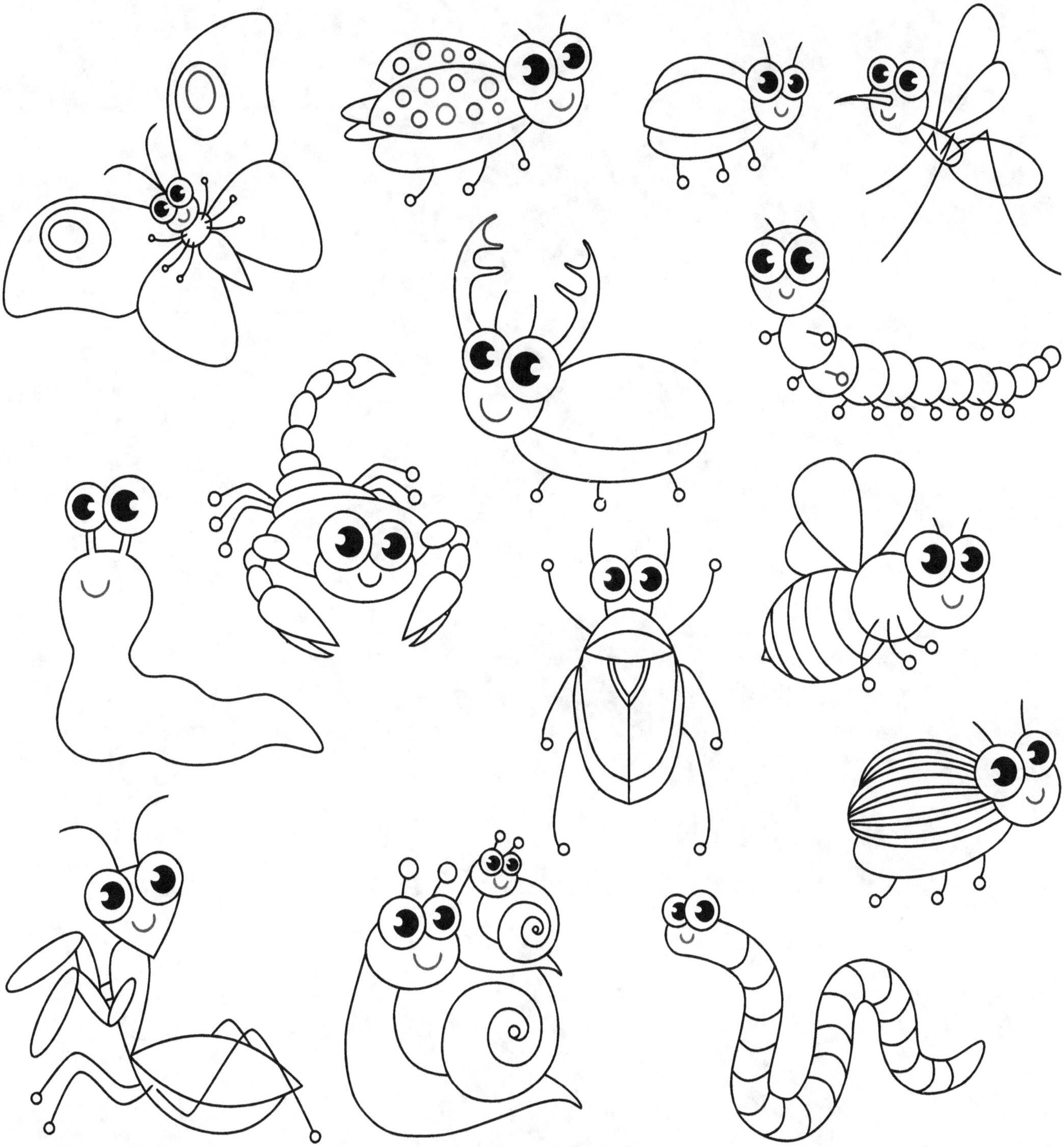

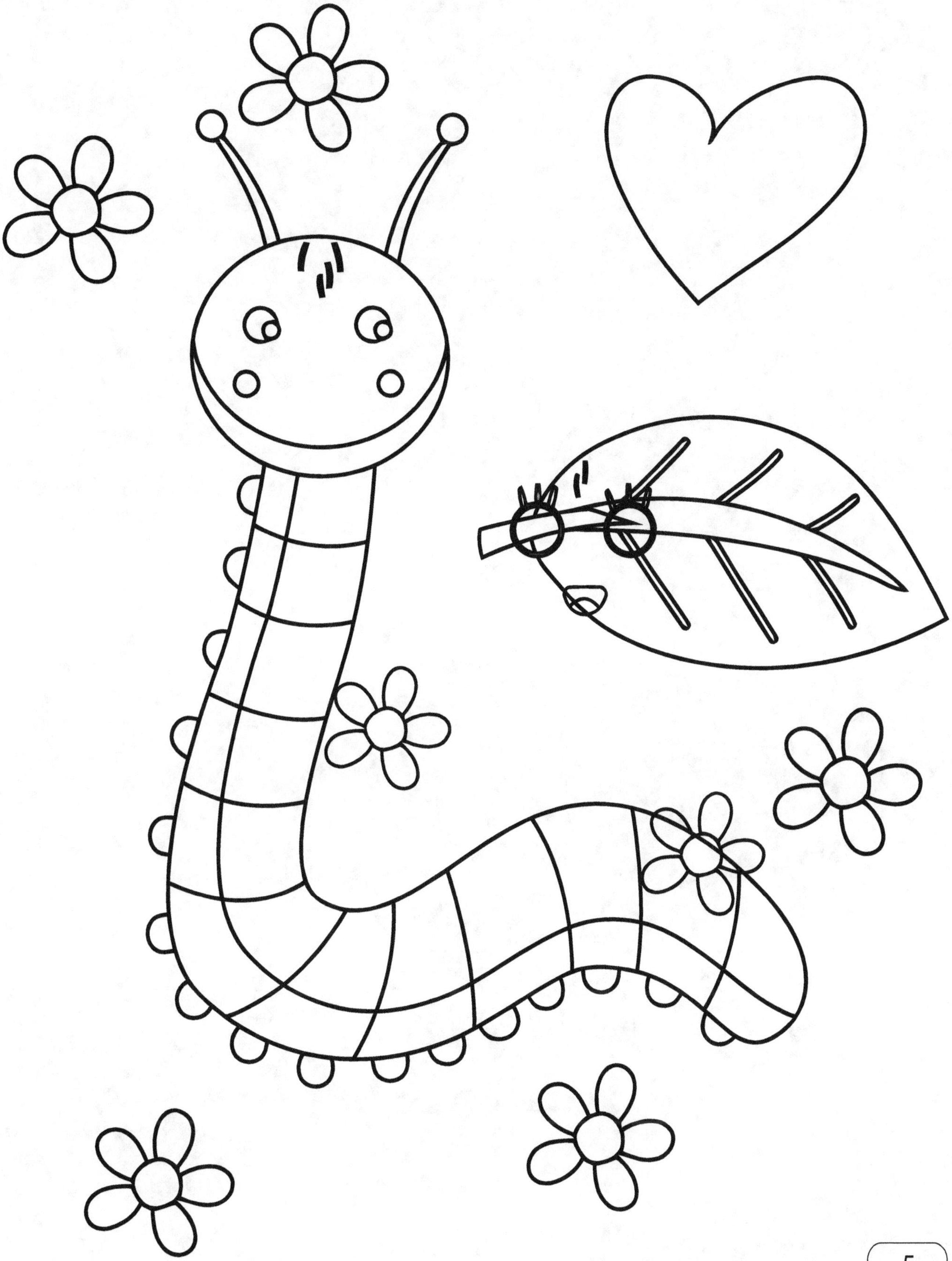

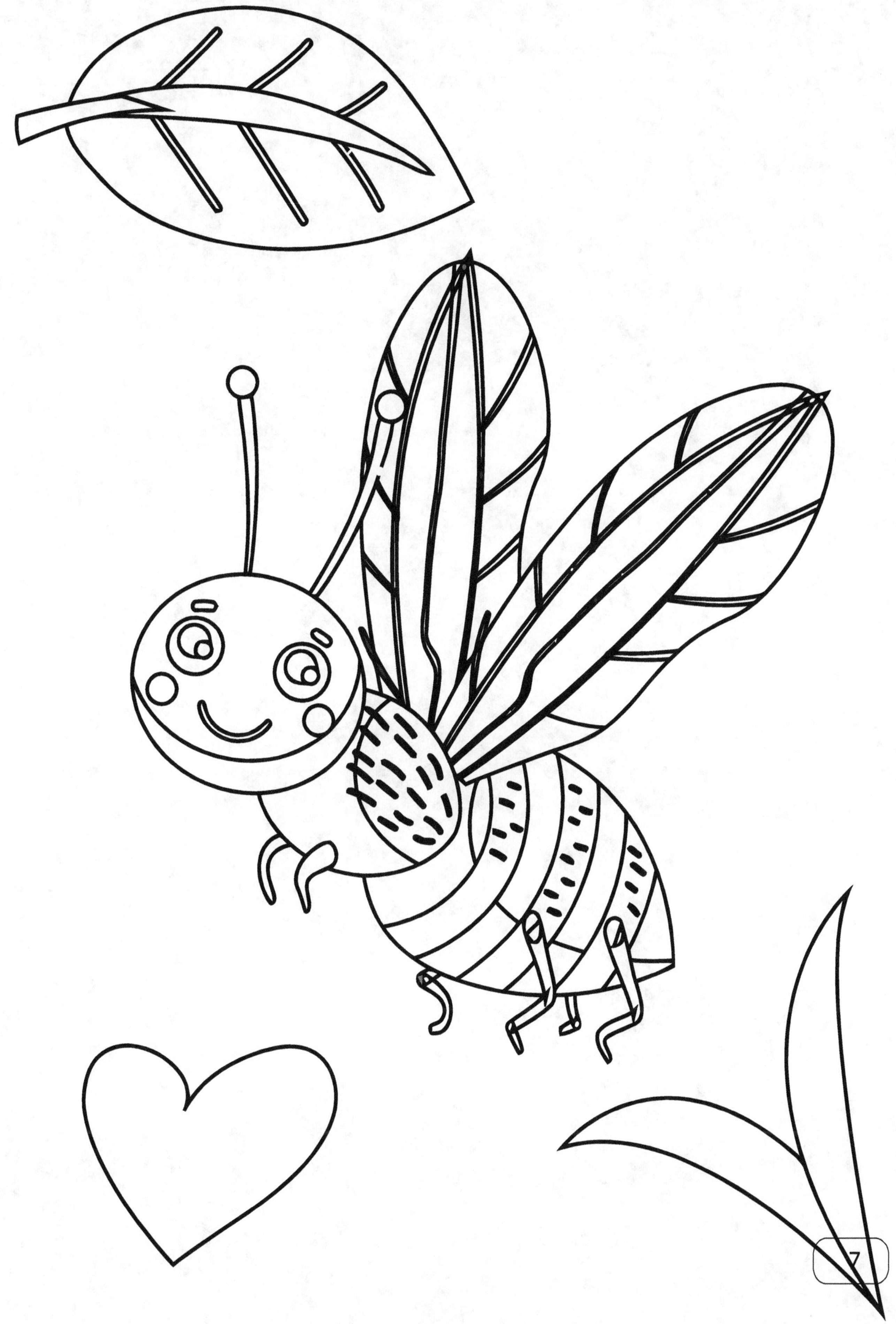

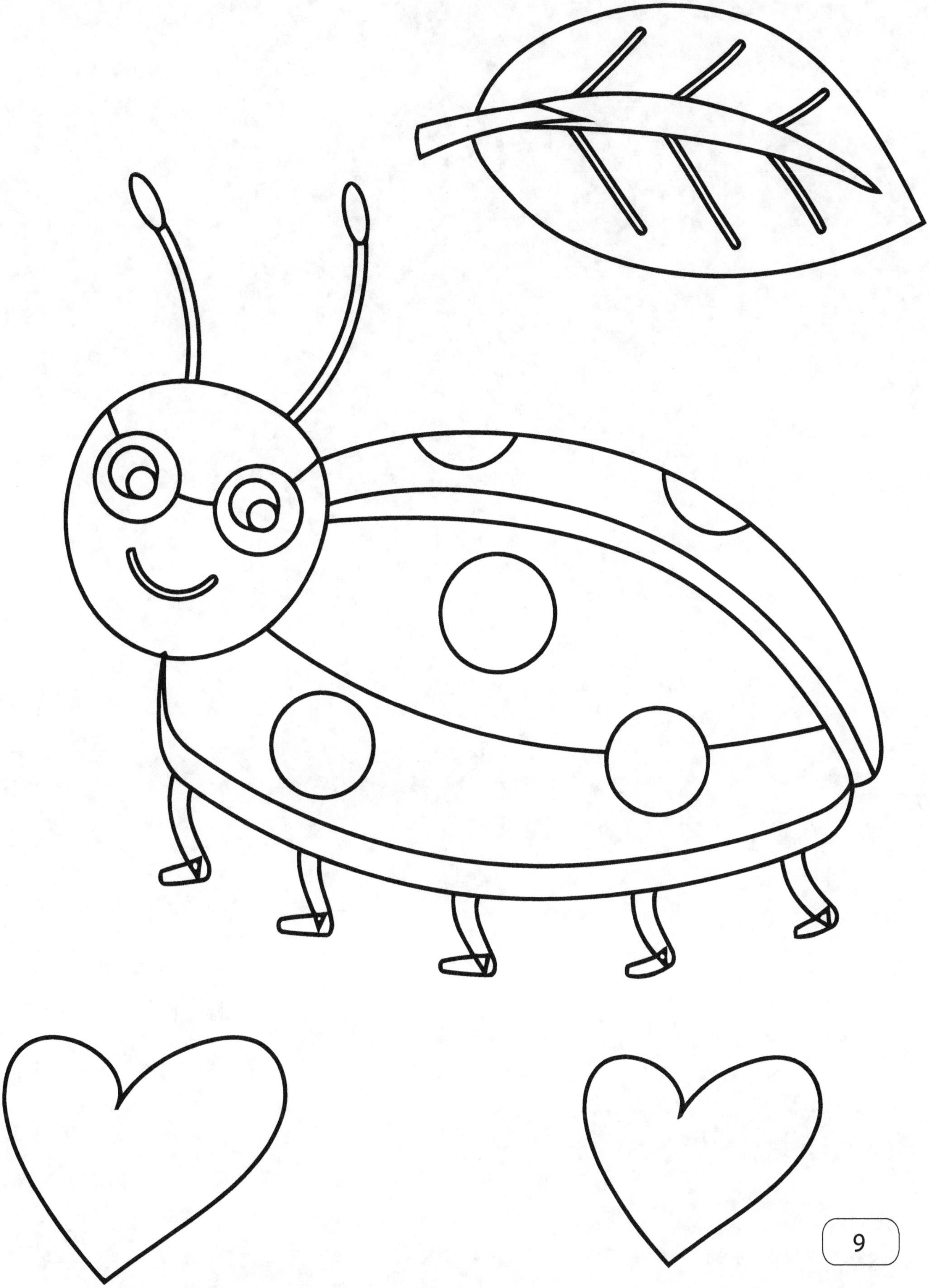

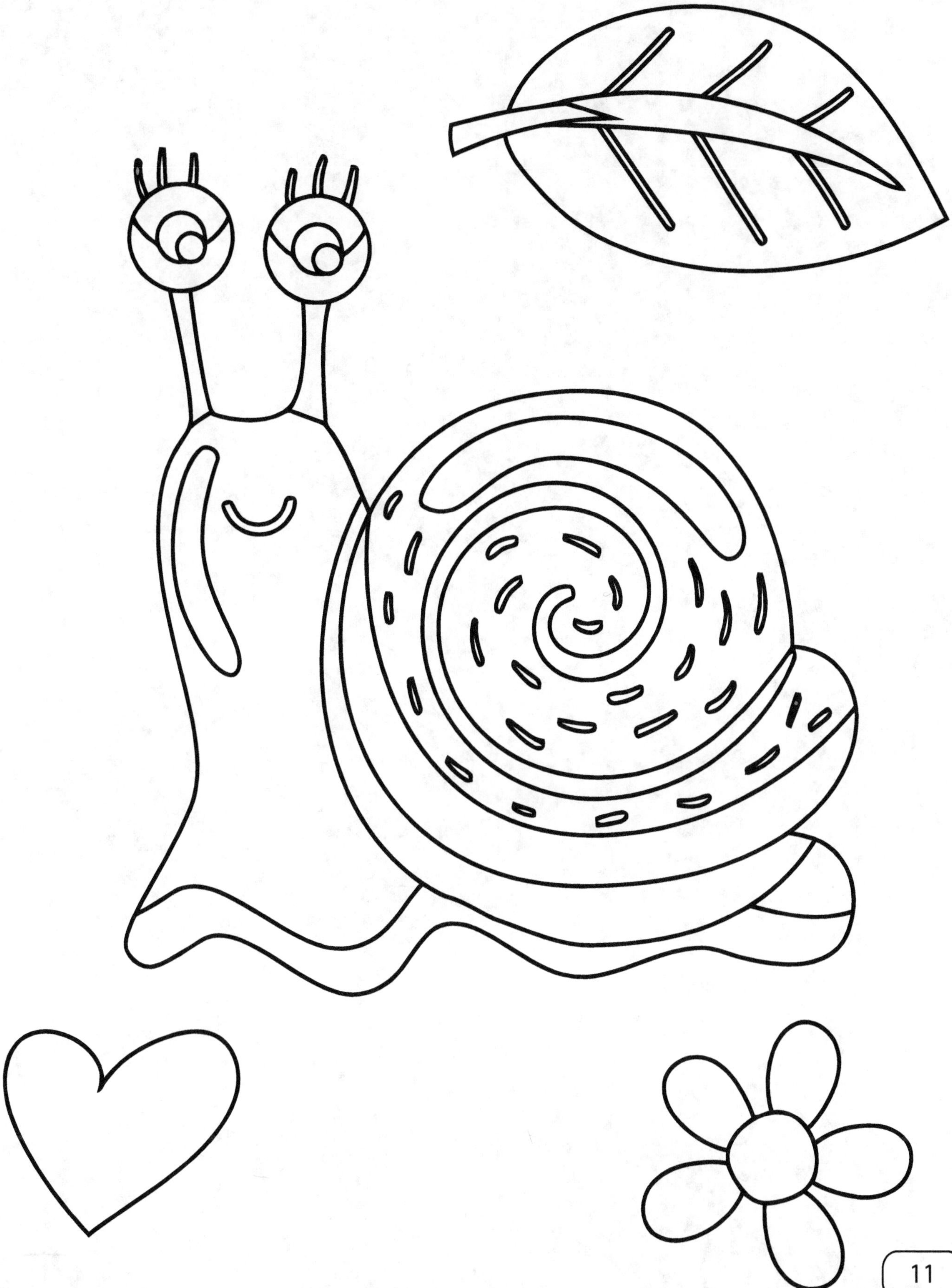

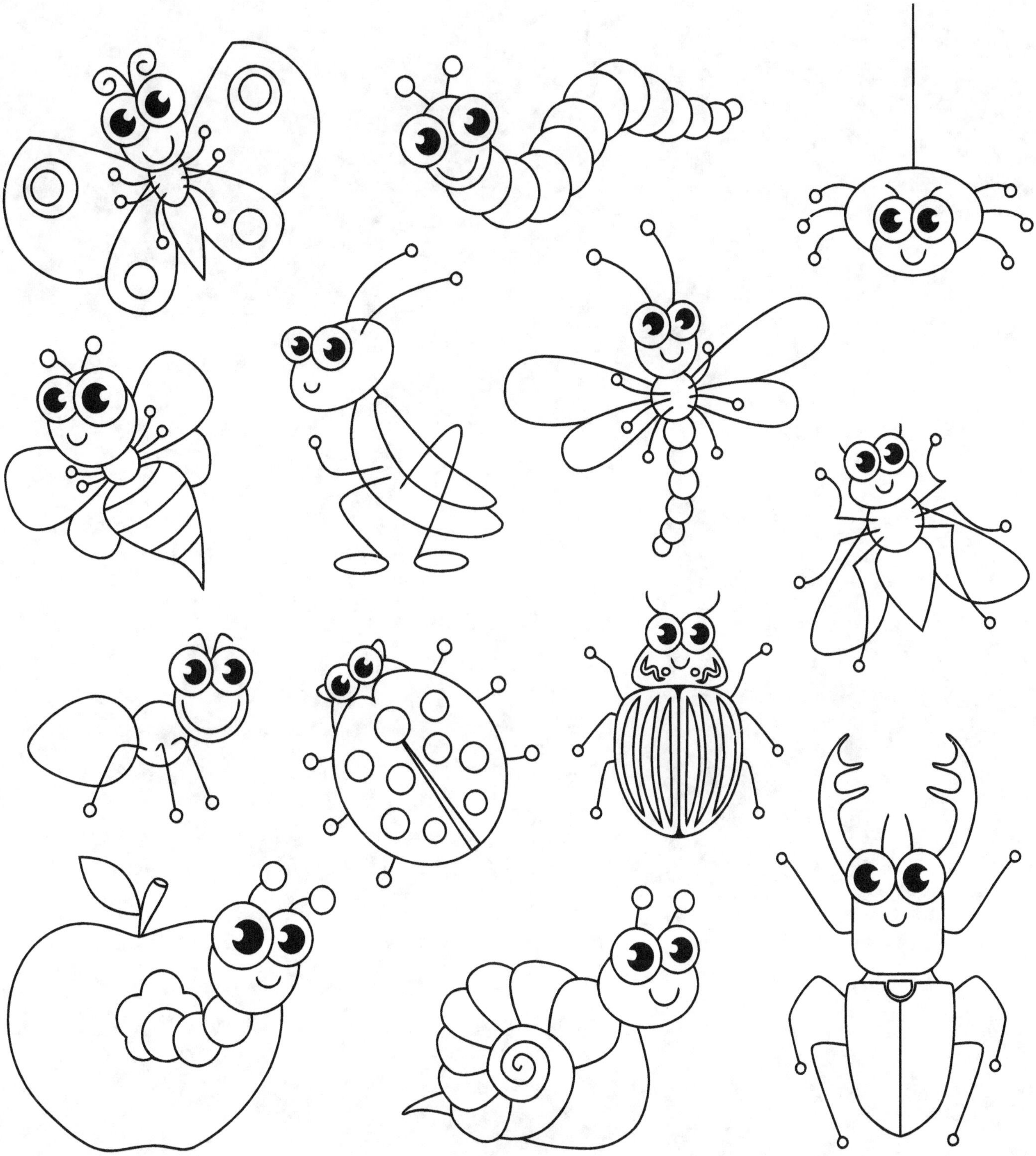

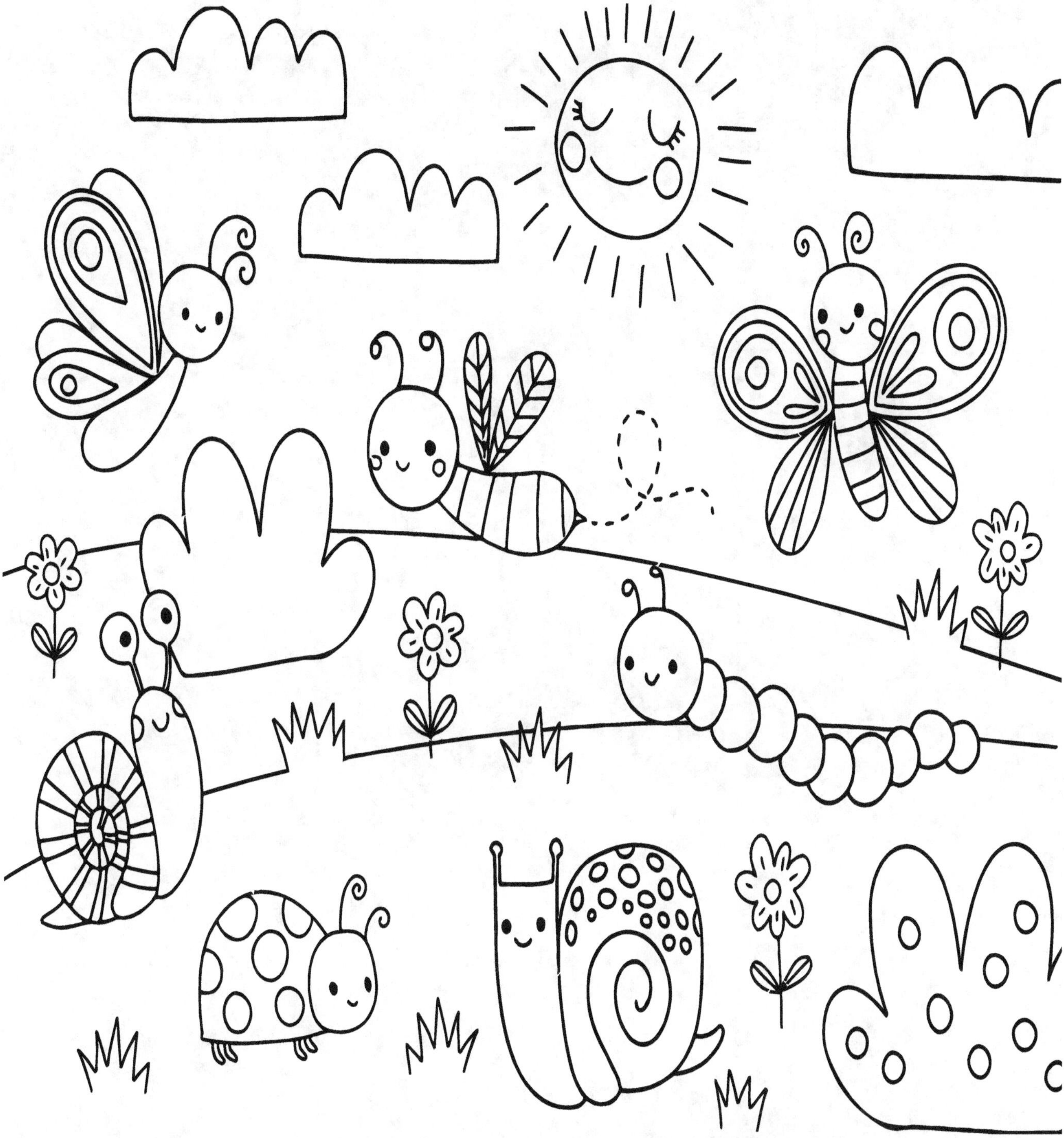

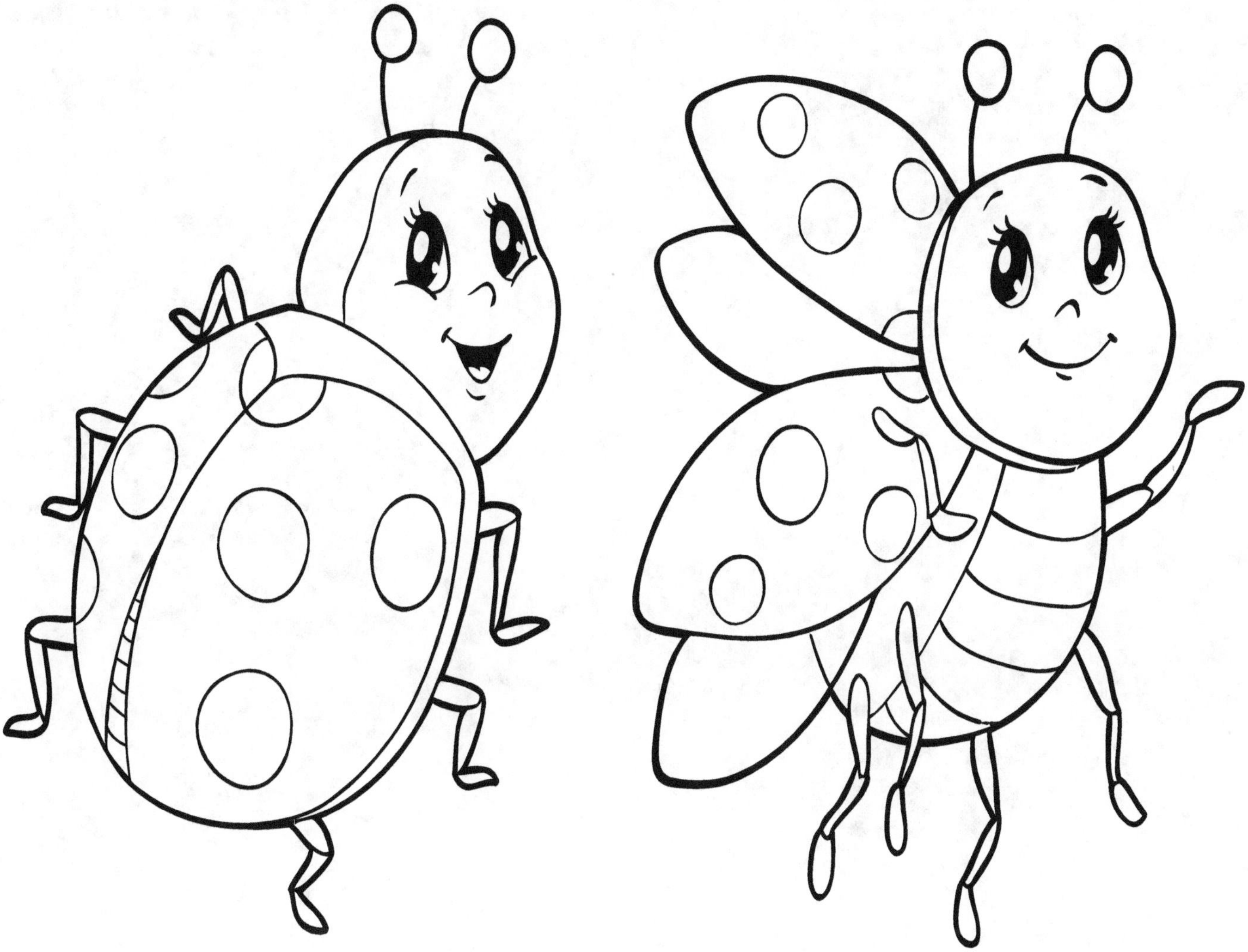

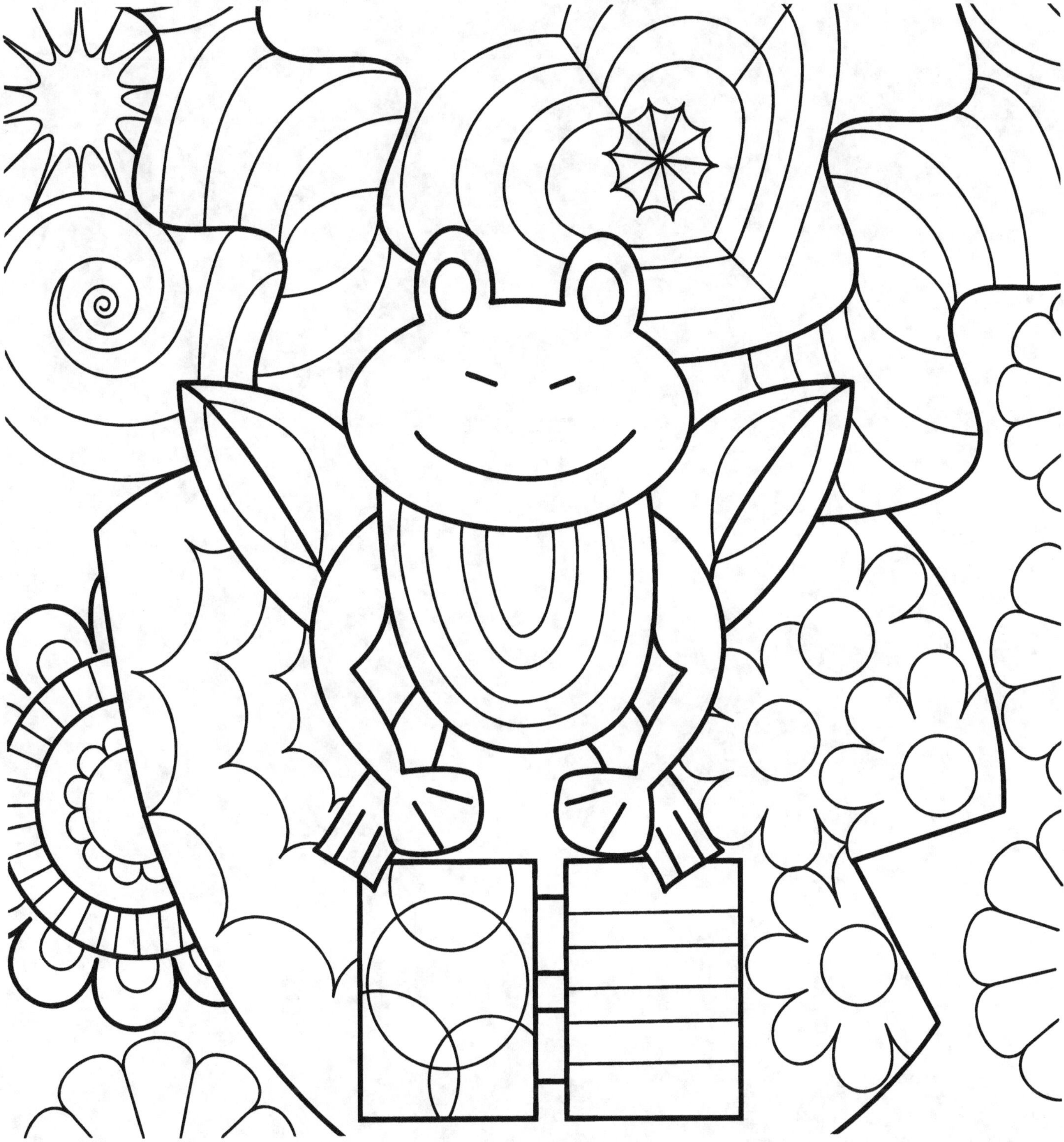

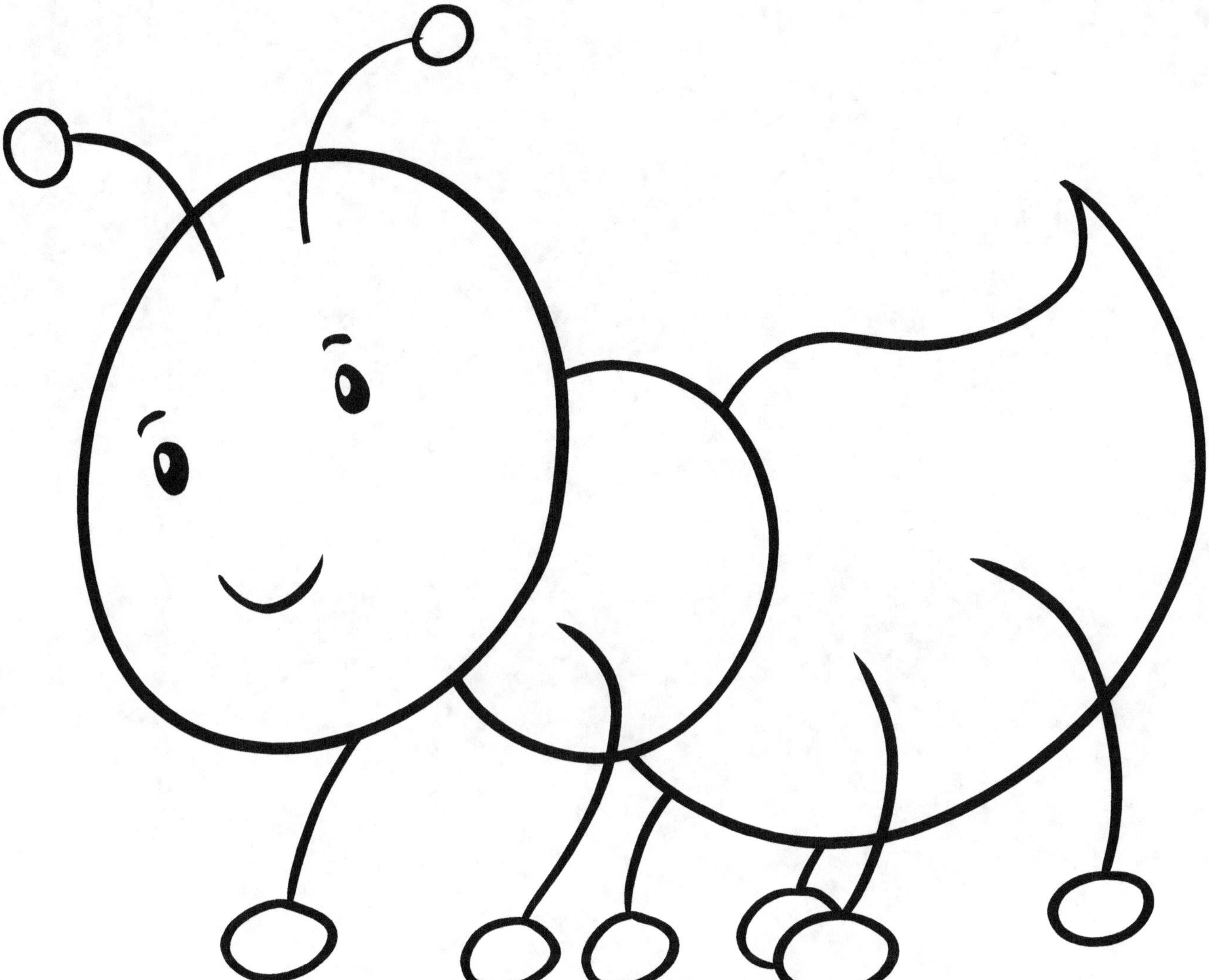

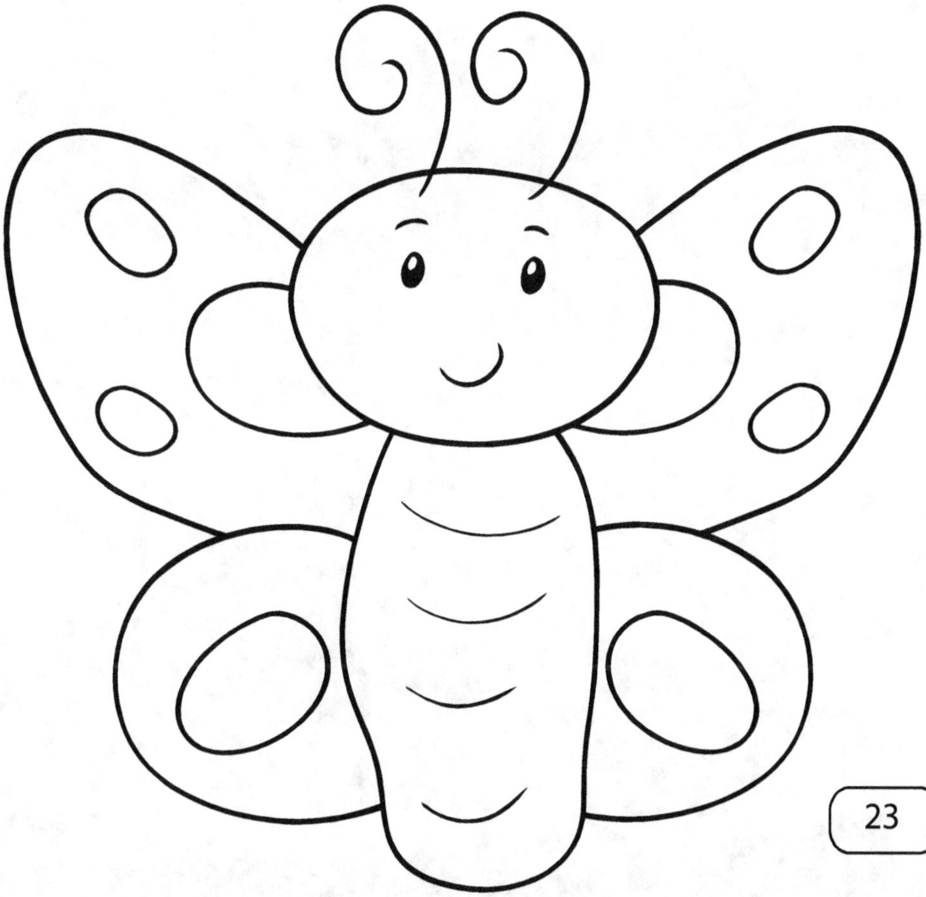

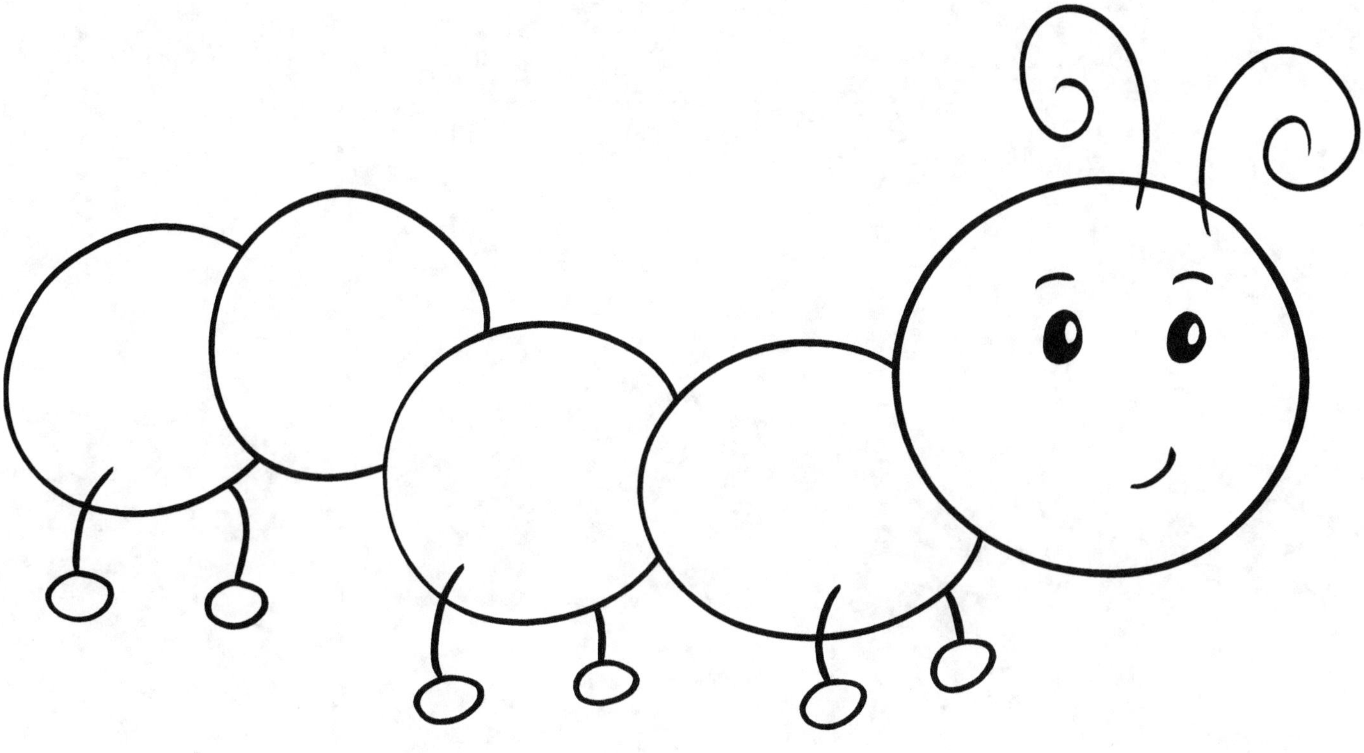

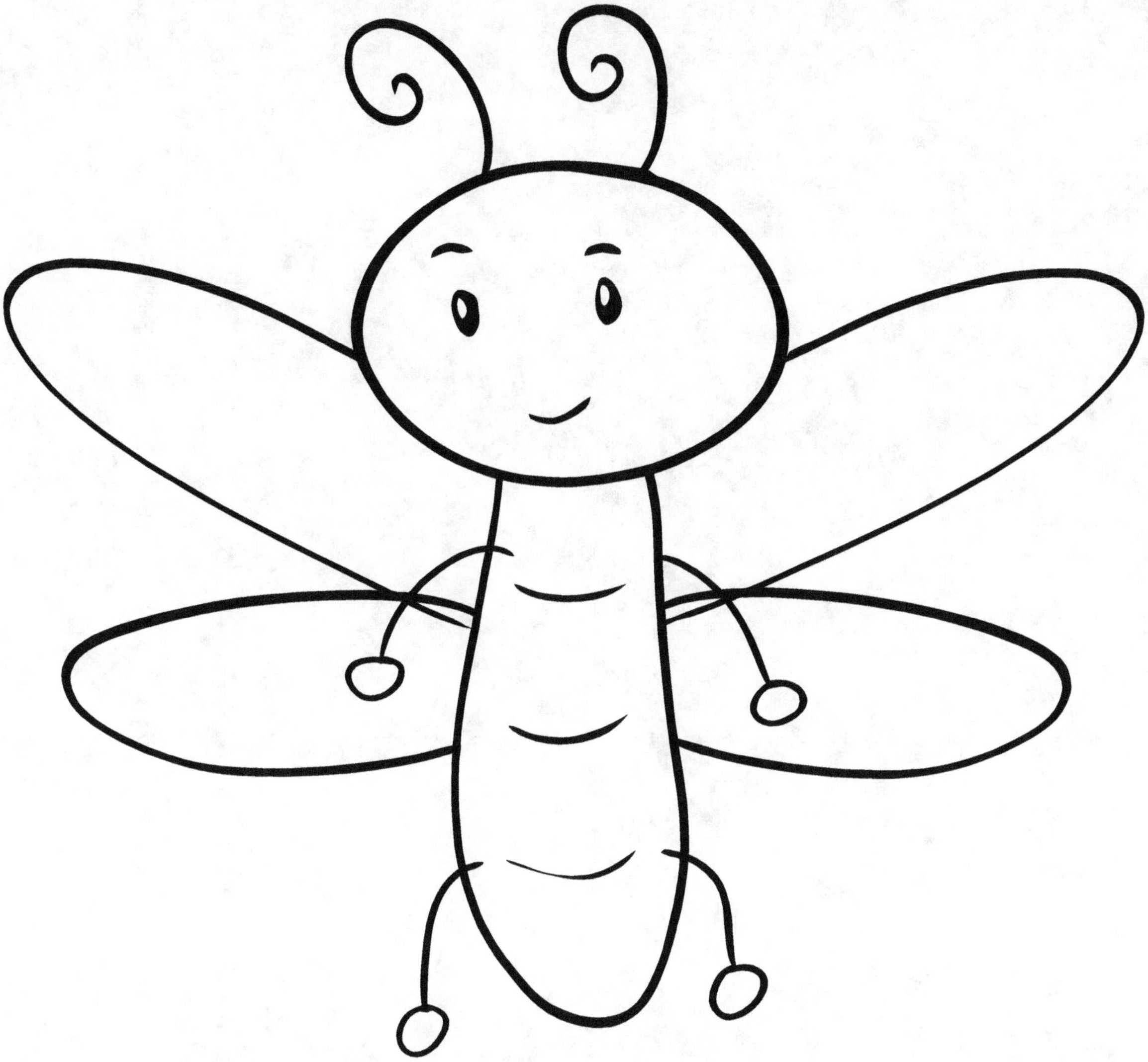

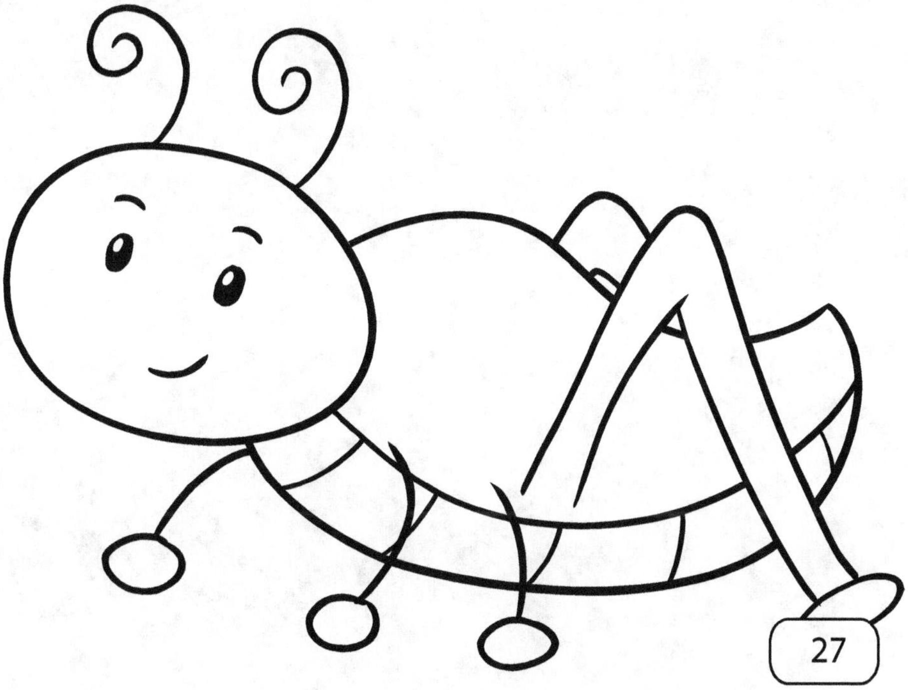

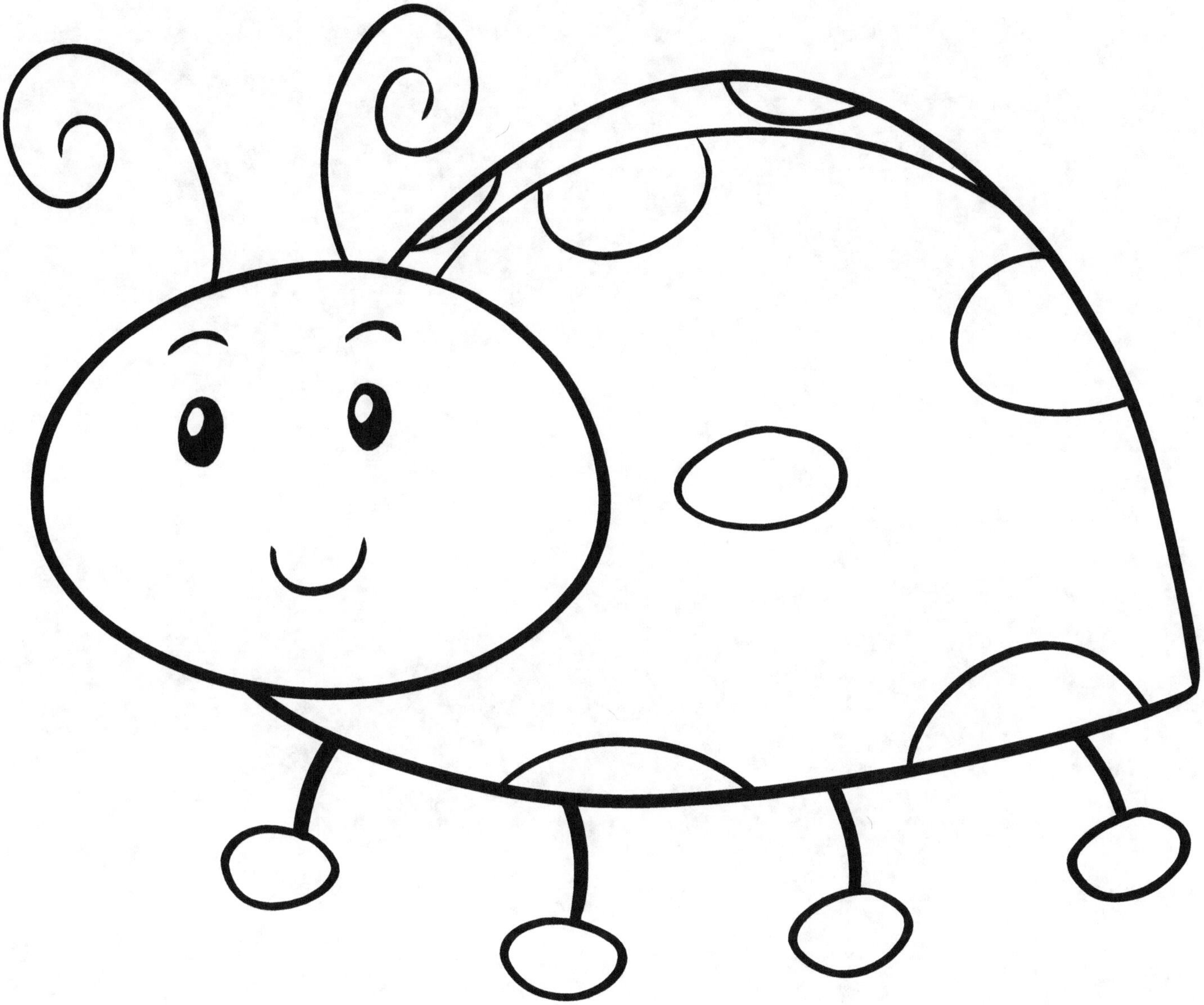

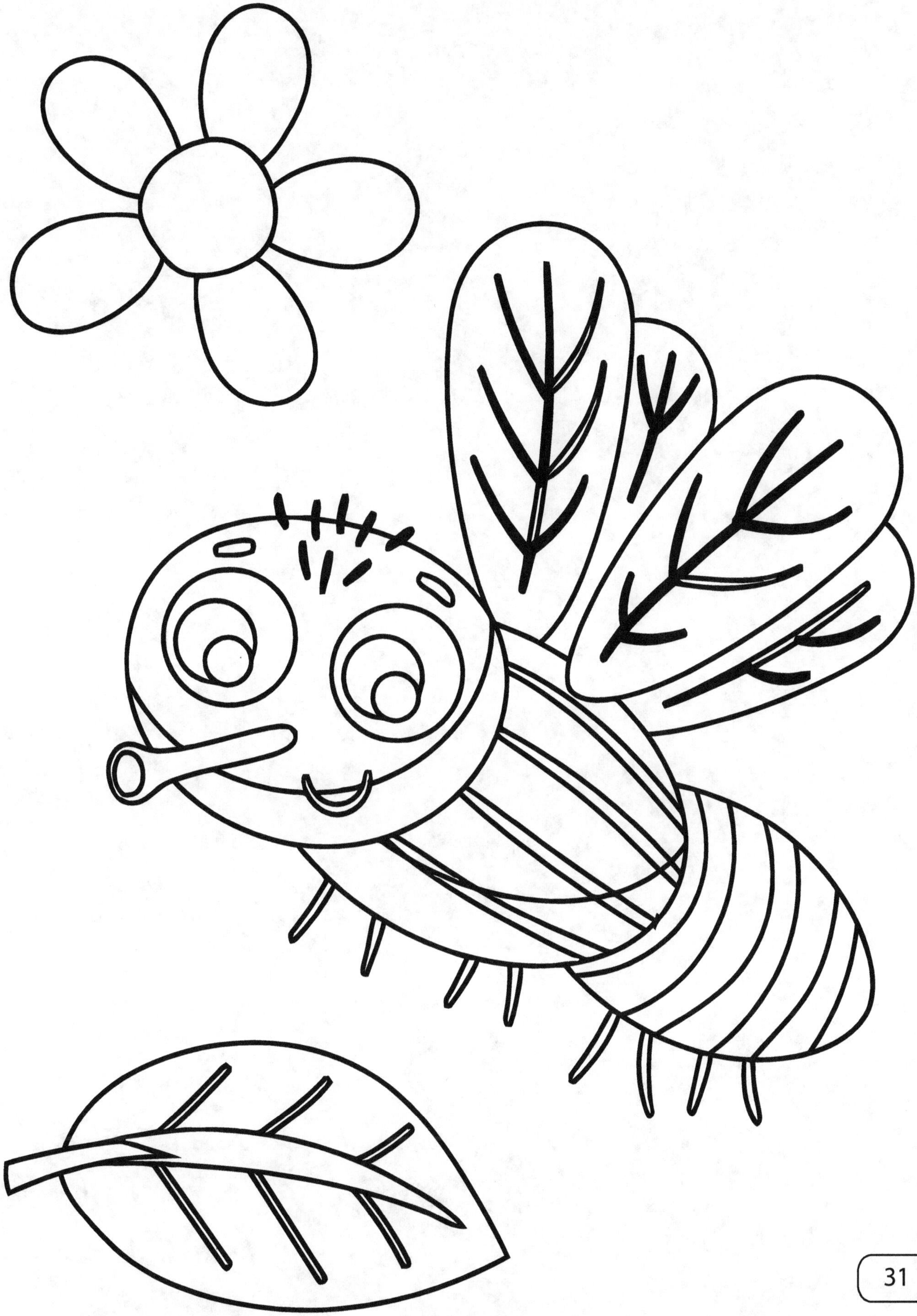

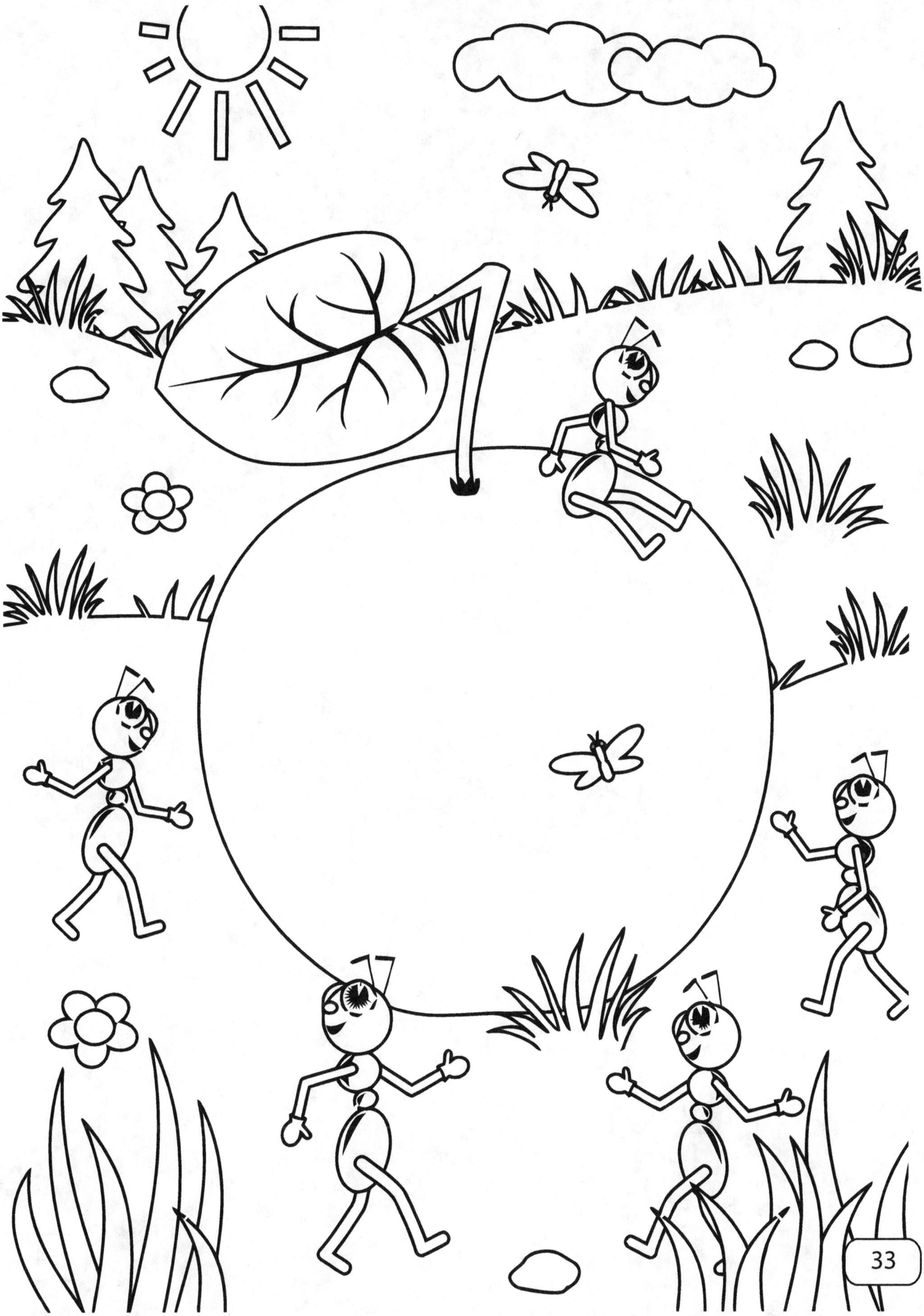

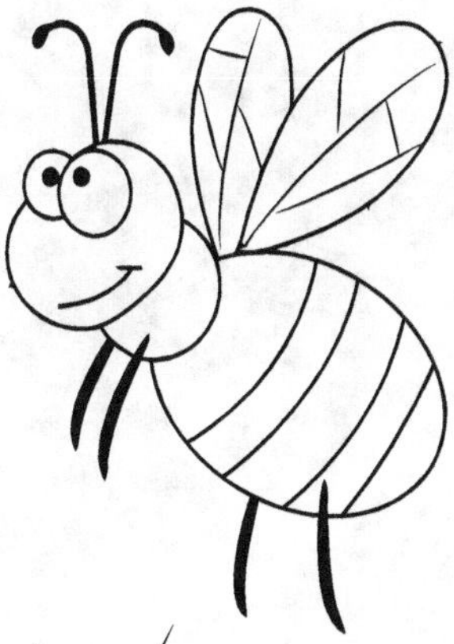
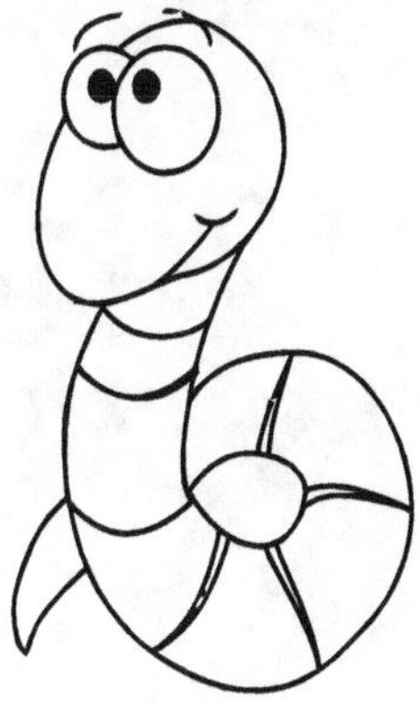
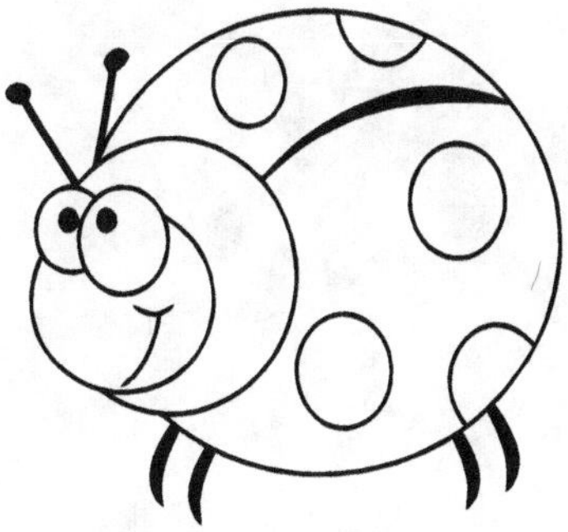
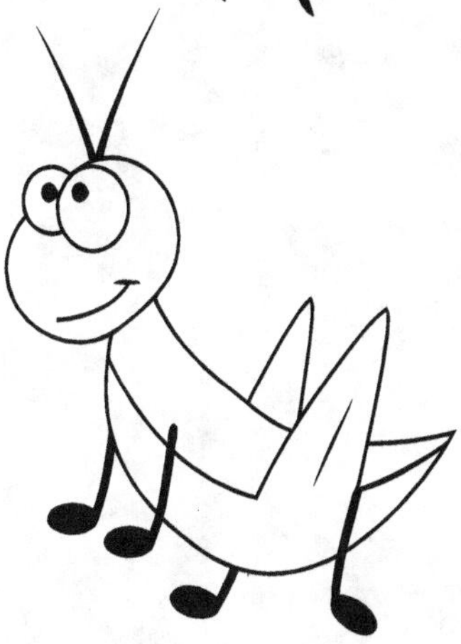
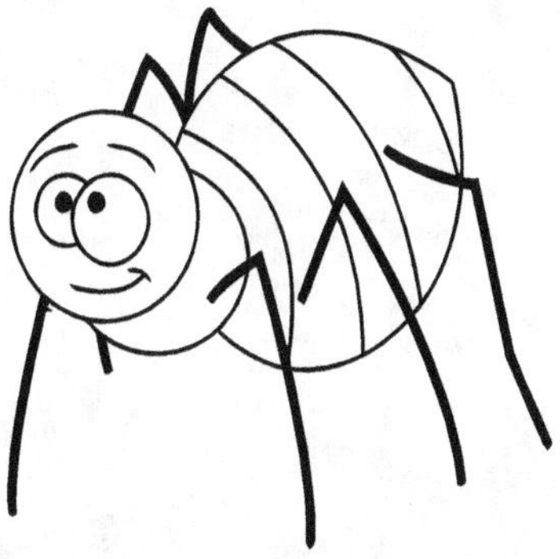
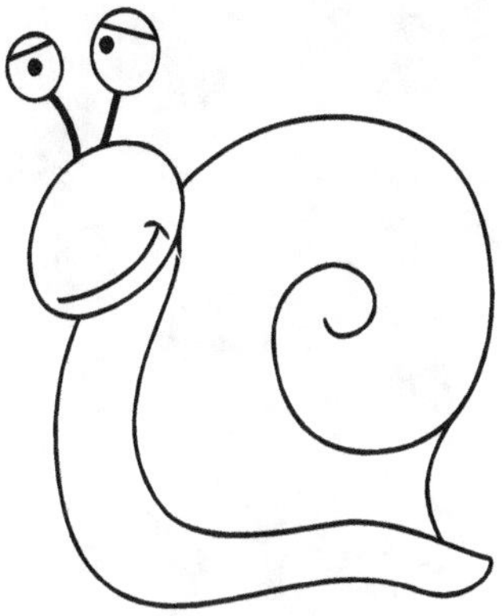
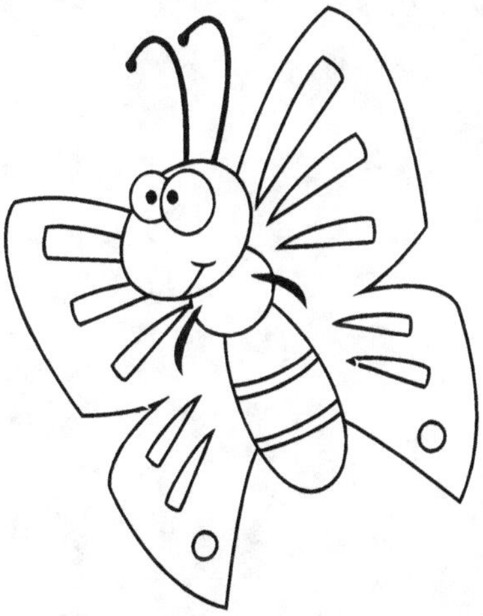
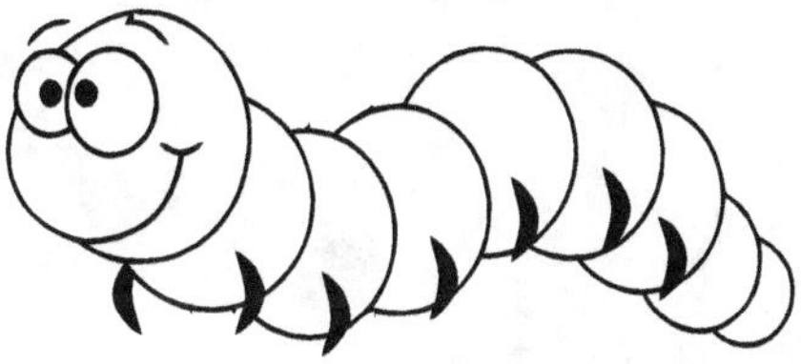
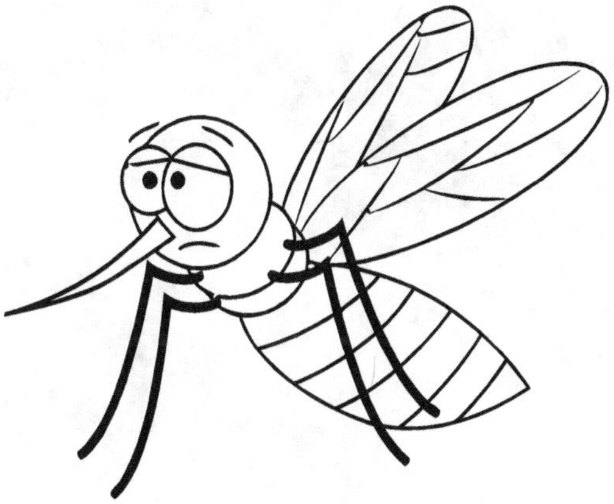

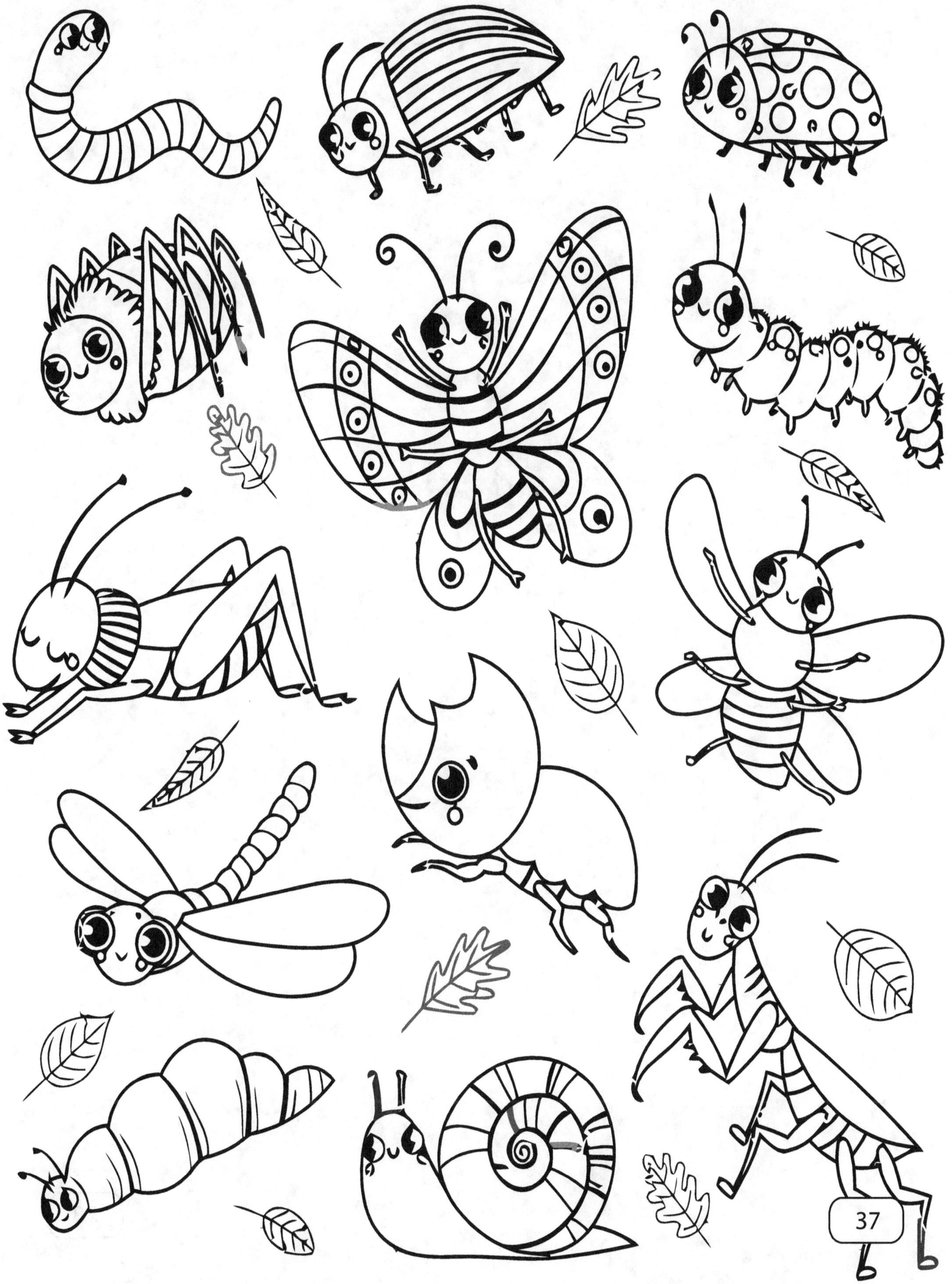

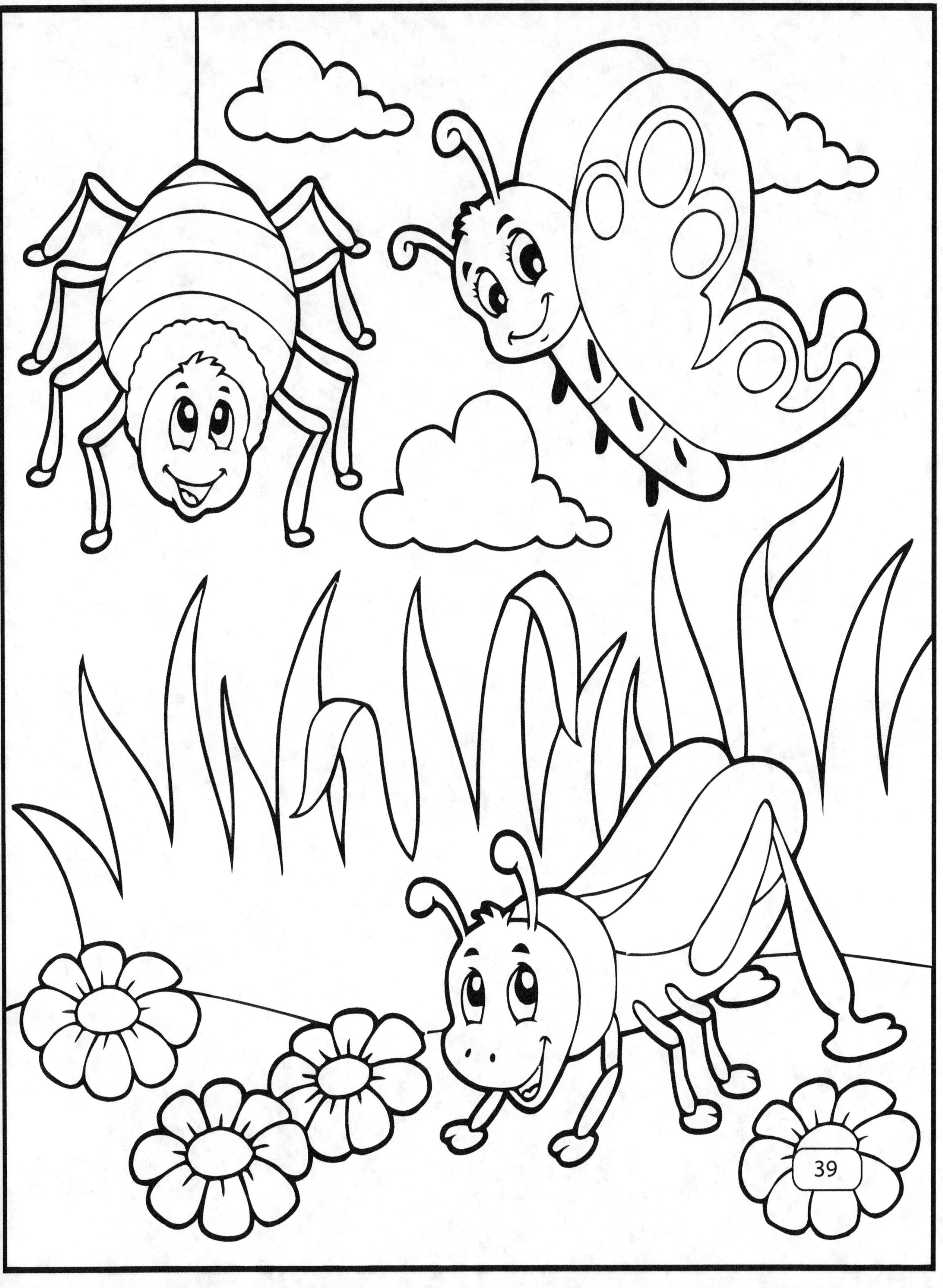

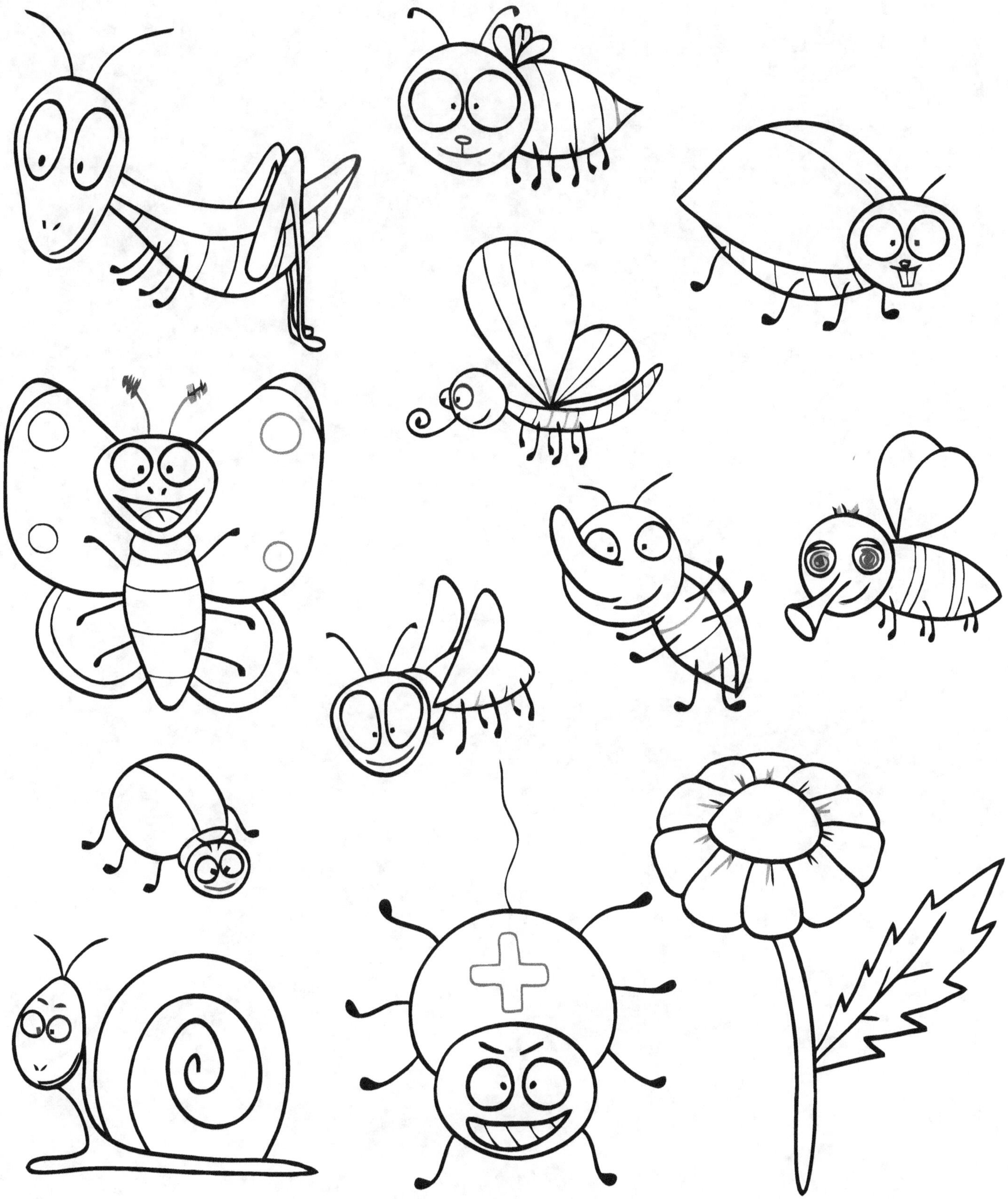

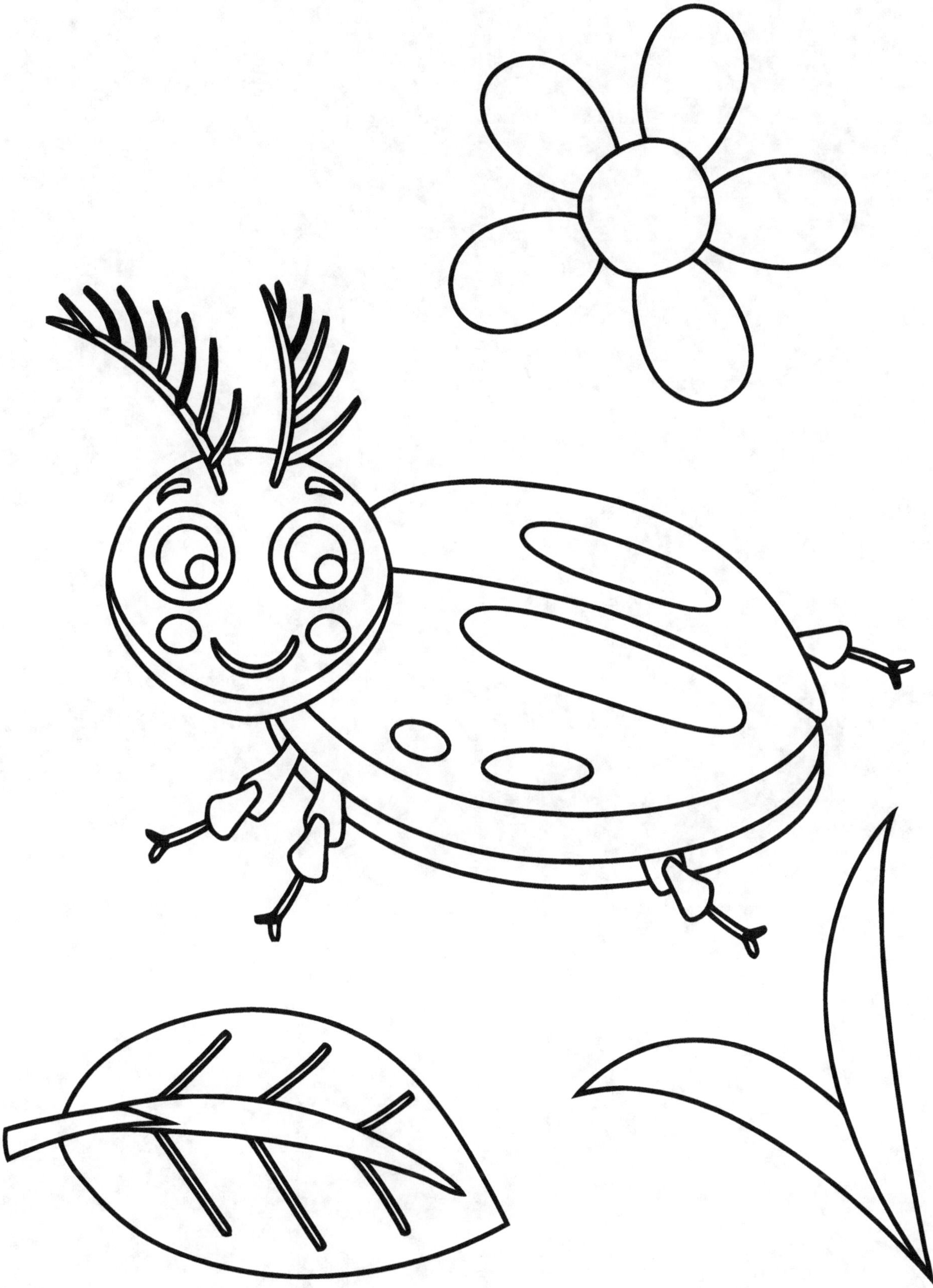

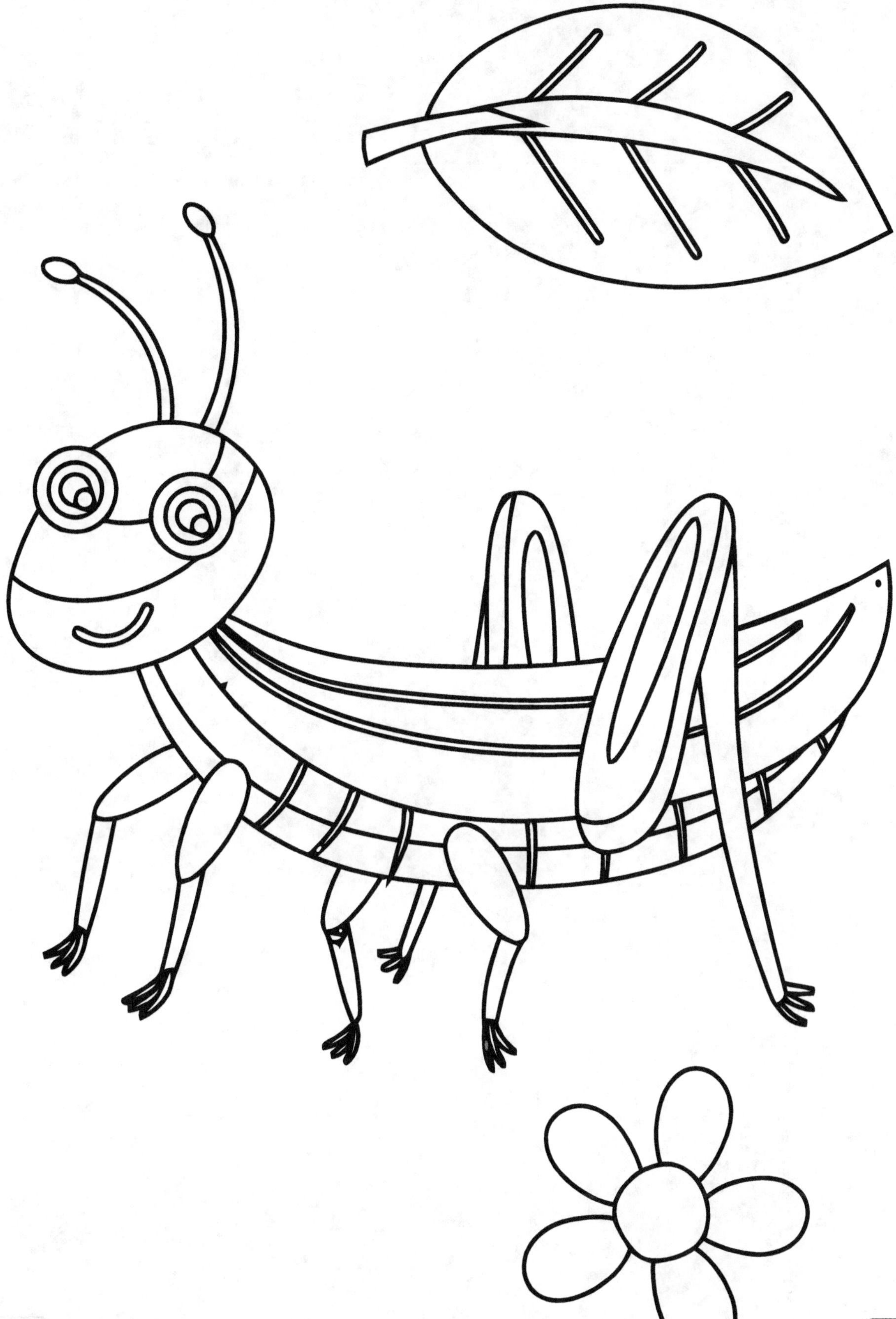

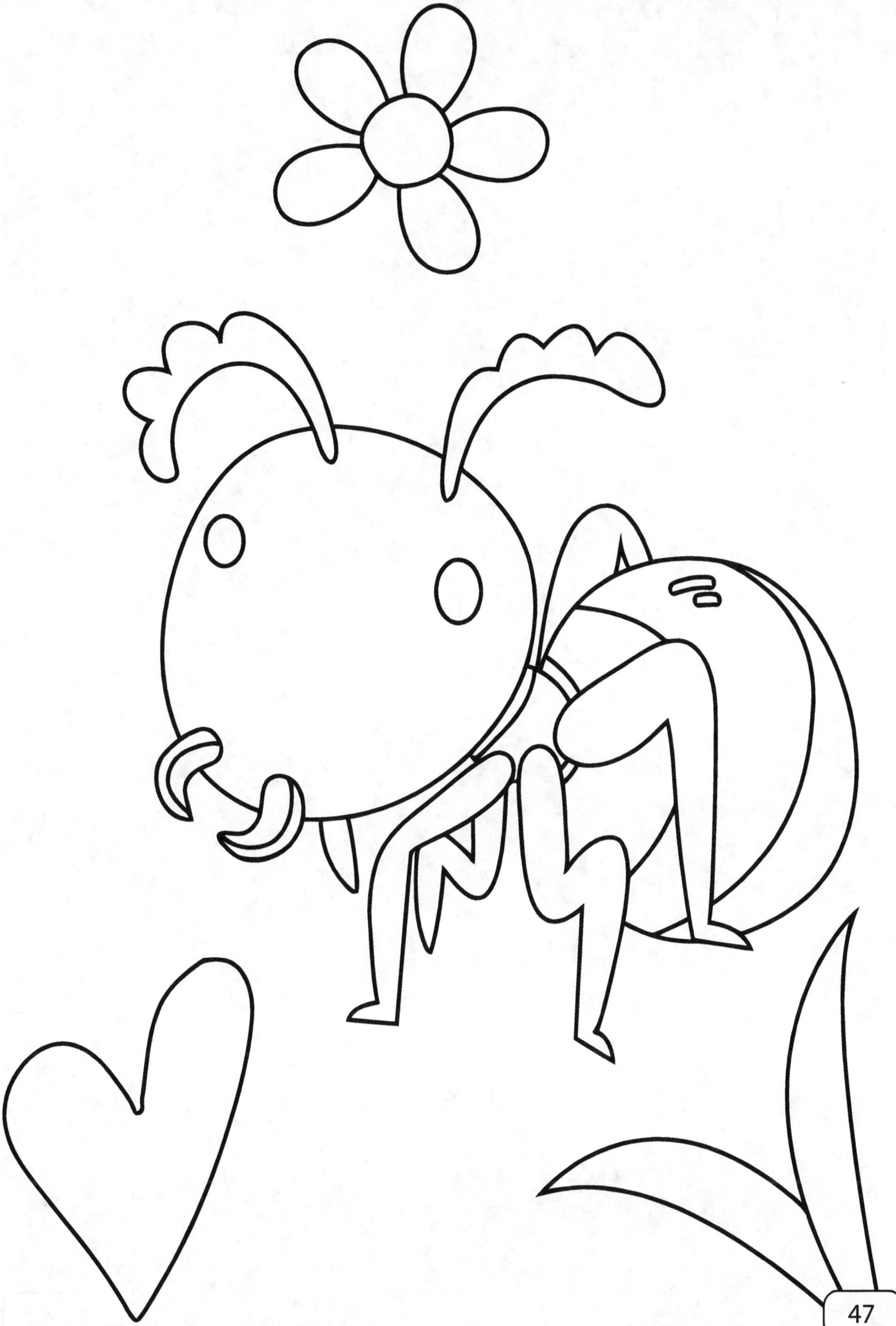

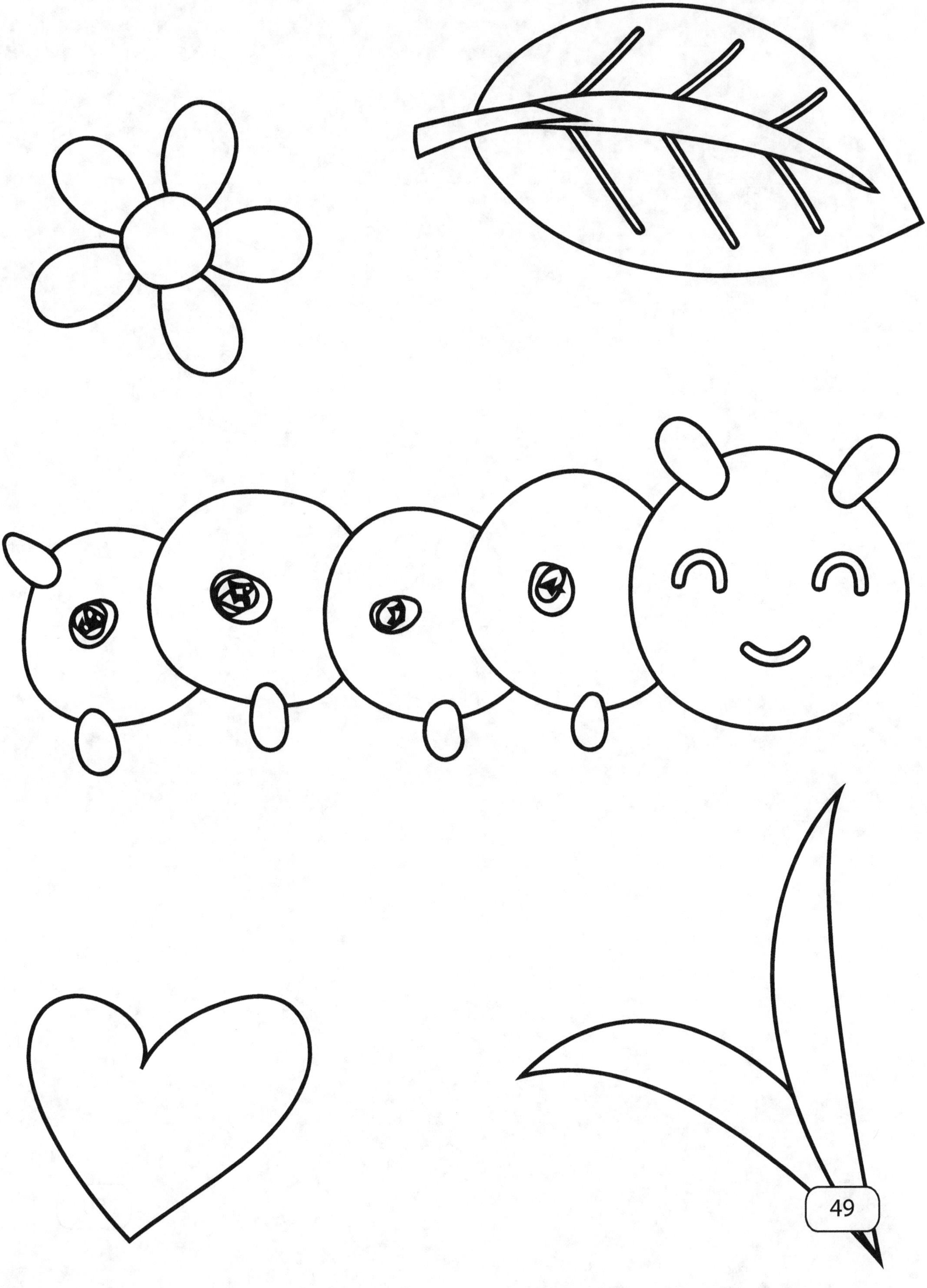

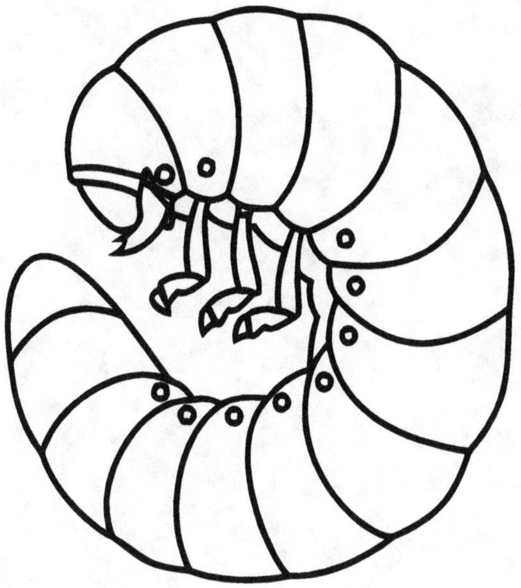

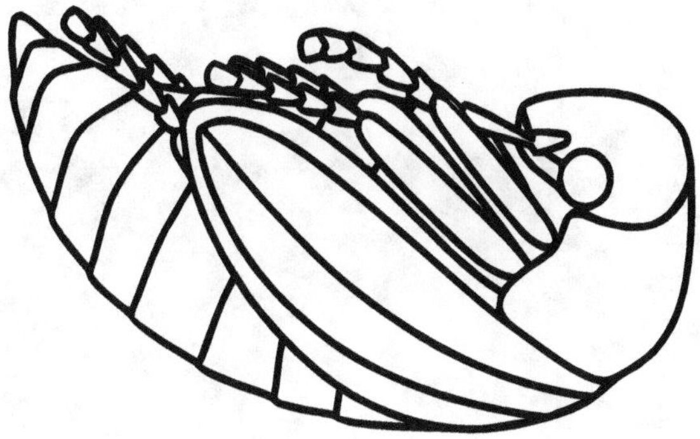

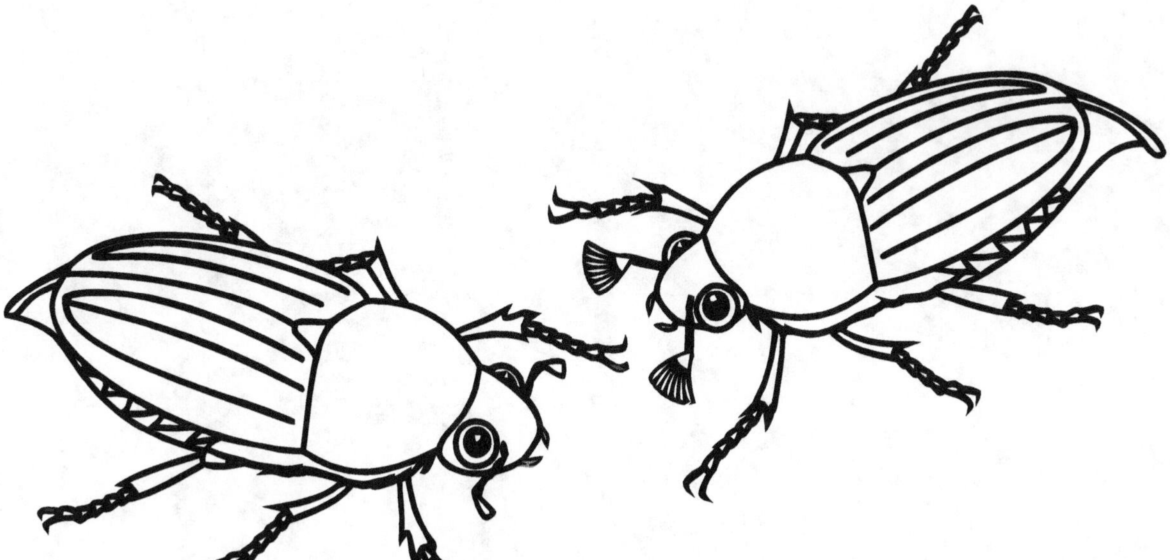

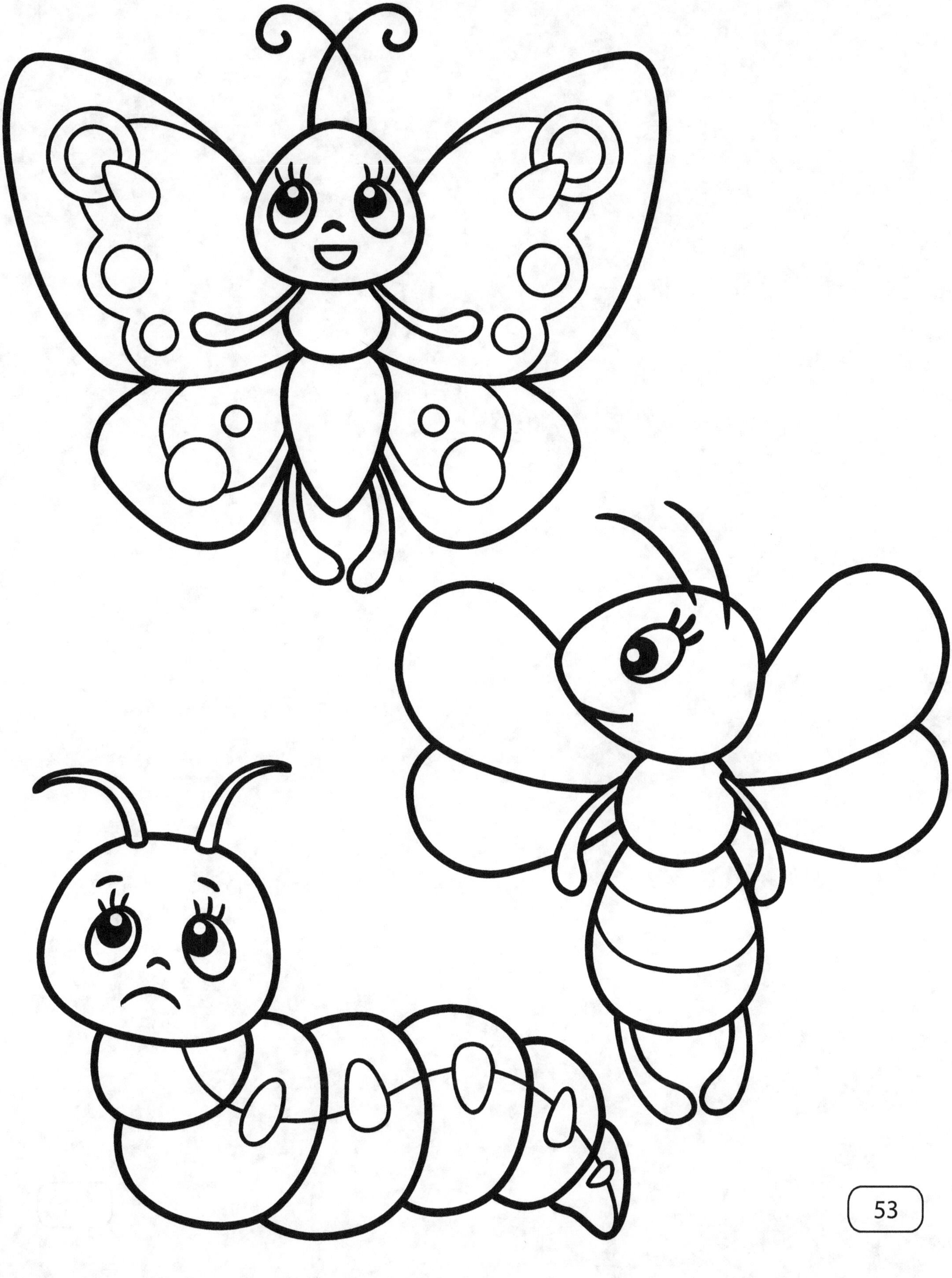

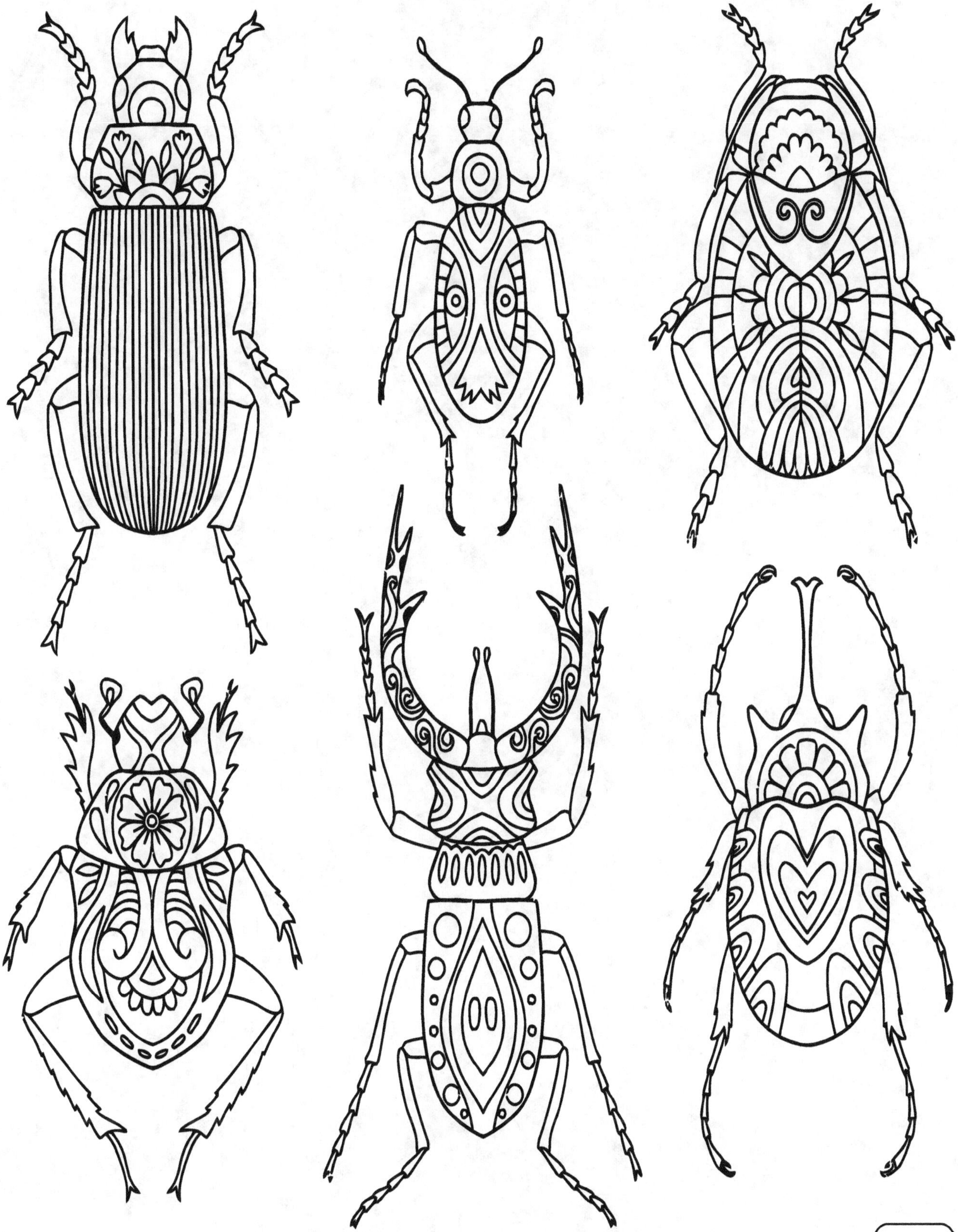

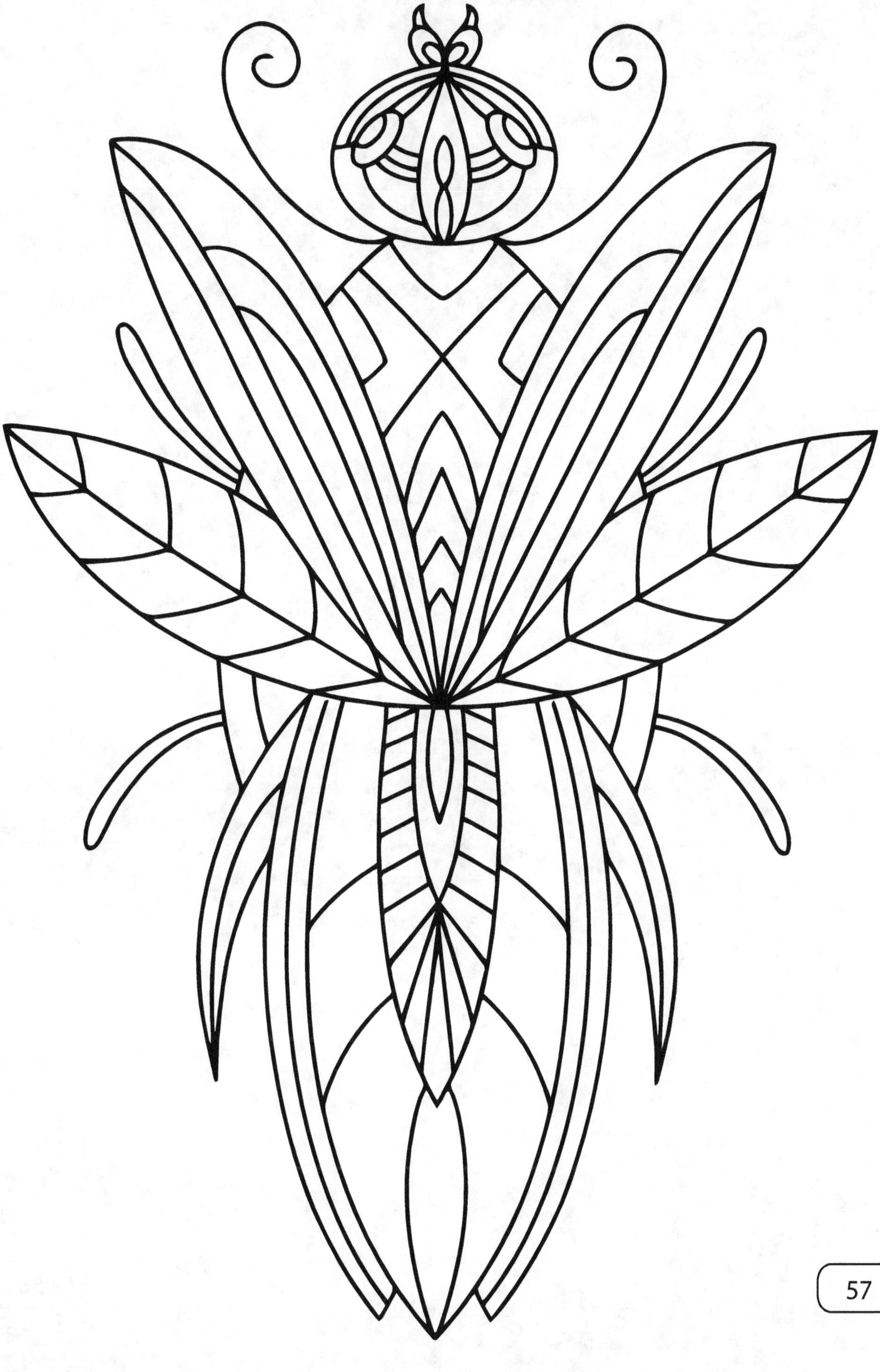

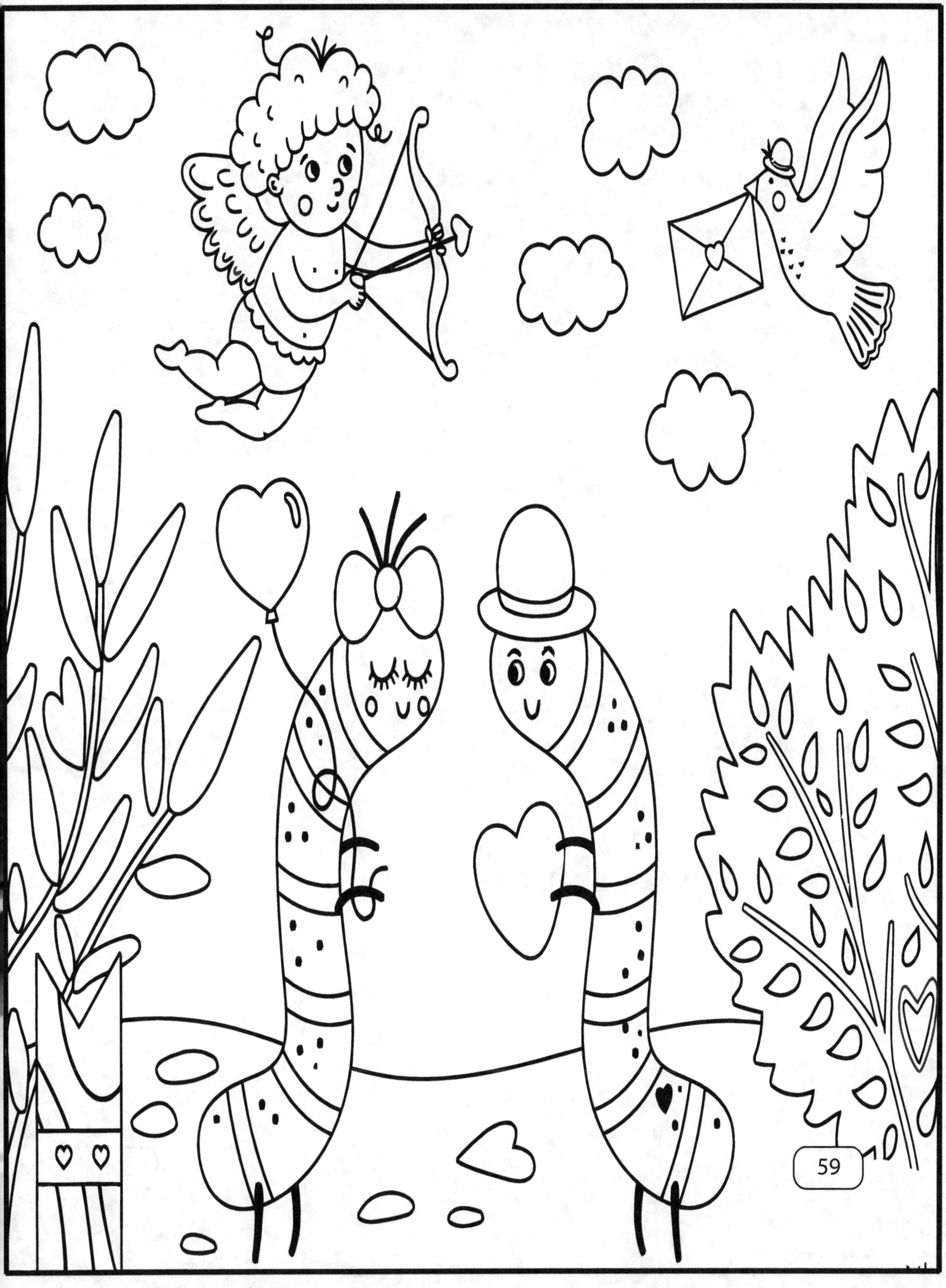